Radical Imagination
Feminist Conceptions of the Future: LeGuin, Piercy, and Gearhart

D1457771

AACHEN BRITISH
AND AMERICAN STUDIES

edited by Richard Martin & Rüdiger Schreyer

Vol./Bd.1

PETER LANG
Frankfurt am Main · Bern · New York · Paris

Margarete Keulen

RADICAL IMAGINATION:
Feminist Conceptions
of the Future
in Ursula Le Guin,
Marge Piercy
and Sally Miller Gearhart

PETER LANG
Frankfurt am Main · Bern · New York · Paris

CIP-Titelaufnahme der Deutschen Bibliothek

Keulen, Margarete:

Radical imagination: feminist conceptions of the future: LeGuin, Piercy, and Gearhart / Margarete Keulen. - Frankfurt am Main ; Bern ; New York ; Paris : Lang, 1991
  (Aachen British and American studies; 1)
  ISBN 3-631-42753-0

NE: GT

ISSN 0721-3980
ISBN 3-631-42753-0

Printed in Germany 1 2 3 4   6 7

I believe we must cope courageously and practically, as women have always done, with the here and now, our feet on this ground where we now live. But nothing less than the most radical imagination will carry us beyond this place, beyond the mere struggle for survival, to that lucid recognition of our possibilities which will keep us impatient, and unresigned to mere survival.

Adrienne Rich

To live well in the present, to live decently and humanely, *we must see into the future*.

Truly, where there is no vision, the people perish.

Robert Scholes

ACKNOWLEDGEMENTS

For the part they played in the completion of this study I am indebted to several friends. My warmest thanks go to Sanjay Laud and Eva Erdpohl for hunting through Californian bookshops (or even the one in the Taj Mahal Hotel in Bombay!) in order to find books which I could not have acquired that easily - if at all; to Brigitte Krause and Eva Erdpohl for suggestions and discussion - and particularly to Eva for her understanding and the occasional pat on the shoulder; to Eva (again!) and Geoffrey V. Davis for reading the manuscript; and to Rüdiger Schreyer for his patience in helping to give it its final shape.

Last, but not least, I want to thank Richard Martin for his encouragement and for making this publication possible.

CONTENTS

PREFACE

> The utopian mode of thought belongs by nature to the realm of theory and speculation. But unlike theory, which seeks knowledge of that which is, the utopian mode of thought is an exercise or plaything with the possibilities lateral to reality . . . it amuses itself in trying out mentally the possibilities which it sees overflowing reality.[1]

This statement by Elisabeth Hansot intimates the complementarity of philosophical and/or political theory and utopian fiction. Consequently, utopian literature is a literature of ideas rather than a literature of aesthetic innovation; the emphasis is on the conceptual rather than on the poetic.

During the last two decades, women writers in the U.S.A. have made increasing use of the utopian mode of thought in their works, particularly in the science fiction genre. Most of these writings may well be regarded as the fictional complement to the New Feminism, which, after having passed through a "phase of programmatic statements," has now reached a state of more self-assurance and opens the ground for exploring new notions of gender.[2] Women writers are stimulated by feminist theory to imagine alternative societies in fiction which challenge and contribute to the present gender discourse and which attempt to translate feminist insights into fictional sociological models. Gisela Ecker therefore thinks that such a work of fiction

> should not be seen as isolated but in the context of wider cultural activities in the production and reception of feminist art and in the context of the general feminist debate. If this larger framework is considered, the liberating value of a single text will surely receive a different interpretation from one which is the result of a separate treatment through literary criticism.[3]

Taking this approach as a point of departure, this study will deal with three novels by contemporary women writers who have developed conceptions of alternative (future) societies: *The Left Hand of Darkness* by Ursula K. LeGuin, *Woman on the Edge of Time* by Marge Piercy, and *The Wanderground* by Sally Miller Gearhart.

---

[1] Elisabeth Hansot, *Perfection and Progress: Two Modes of Utopian Thought* (Cambridge, Mass.: MIT Press, 1974) p. 13.
[2] Gisela Ecker, "The Politics of Fantasy in Recent American Women's Novels," *Englisch-Amerikanische Studien*, 3 (1984) p. 510.
[3] *ibid.*, p. 509.

11

1. INTRODUCTION

1.1   The Literary Tradition of Imaginative Models of Society: A Short Survey

Imaginative models of society - ideal or future - have a very long tradition in Western thought and literature. Within the scope of this study I cannot attempt a thorough survey of the many works in this tradition.[1] I therefore shall focus on the most important and best known works and outline the designs of societies they contain, paying special attention to the role of women.

* * *

Plato's *Republic* (fourth century B.C.) is usually regarded as the pioneer work in this tradition, the "prototype of what later came to be known as utopian literature."[2] Plato designed the "good" society on the basis of reason and rationality. He foresaw an elite ruling class, the Guardians, who were supposed to live communally. Traditional family ties were to be abolished among them as these only led to private interests and private property which were to be abolished, too. Thus it was ensured that the individual's loyalty and energy would be entirely directed toward the group and its well-being. This rather radical proposal was picked up again much later in utopian and dystopian literature; it was also included in the plans of many so-called "intentional communities" of the nineteenth and twentieth centuries in the U.S.A.[3]

In order to maintain the elitist qualities of the leadership group, Plato included eugenic regulations. Sexual relations were only allowed at certain public festivals ("hymeneals") between predetermined partners.

These ideas about the abolition of the nuclear family and the regulation of sexuality entailed major changes in the social order, particularly for women.

---

[1] As a survey of utopian writing and its criticism and commentary see for instance Julio A. Martinez, "General Bibliographies," in E.D.S. Sullivan, ed. *The Utopian Vision: Some Essays on the Quincentennial of Sir Thomas More* (San Diego: San Diego State University Press, 1983) pp. 177-233; Gorman Beauchamp, "Themes and Uses of Fictional Utopias: A Bibliography of Secondary Works in English," *Science Fiction Studies*, 4 (1977) pp. 55-63.

[2] Daphne Patai, "Utopia for Whom," *Aphra*, 5,3 (1974) p. 4. For a further discussion of Plato's *Republic* in the light of this study cf. also Elaine Hoffman Baruch, "'A Natural and Necessary Monster': Women in Utopia," *Alternative Futures* (1979) pp. 30-32; Lyman Tower Sargent, "Women in Utopia," *Comparative Literature Studies*, 10,1 (1973) p. 303.

[3] For the definition of "intentional communities" as a group in which the primary bond among members is other than blood or legal, see Batya Weinbaum, "Twin Oaks: A Feminist Looks at Indigenous Socialism in the United States," in Rohrlich and Baruch, eds., *Women in Search of Utopia* (New York: Schocken Books, 1984) p. 160.

As household duties had become a communal task, women were no longer restricted to the domestic realm. Children were to be raised collectively in 14 "nurseries". The women would not know which of the children were theirs, and would suckle any child. Otherwise, they were free to participate in the same activities as men in the life of the Guardians. They could hunt, fight, and so forth. Plato used analogies from animal life, particularly dogs, to justify his unique point of view that apart from the fact that they bear children, women are no different from men, i.e. the biological difference does not necessitate a different nature in woman. For a very long time Plato was the only Western thinker and author to grant women such equality in the political and sexual realm, membership in the highest ruling class and the right to equal education.

Although Plato views women as just as capable as men, he nevertheless thinks them inherently inferior and not quite as good as men except in the traditionally feminine domains of cooking and needlework, in which they might even excell. Furthermore, there are some privileges in the sexual realm for particularly brave young male Guardians.

On the whole, Plato's *Republic* is a rather rigidly controlled society in which group interests rank higher than those of the individual and emotion and passion are seemingly ruled out. Compared to the various conceptions of alternative and ideal societies which were to be written during the following centuries, the place Plato assigned woman in his plan is rather high. He also established a paradigm that was left unshaken for a long time to come, namely that for women to become equal, they must in a way become "men", i.e. join in masculine activities. This reveals the point of view that women and their traditional activities are in fact regarded as inferior and uninteresting.

* * *

The next important work in this tradition is Thomas More's *Utopia* (1516), which gave its name to the genre.[4] Whereas Plato's *Republic* was a philosophical tract, *Utopia* is a fictional work embedded in the frame of a travel tale. Nevertheless it is firmly rooted in Christian humanism, which leads to major differences in the design of the good society. More's utopian people live mostly communally (eating arrangements, work), have little interest in private property and wealth, and have achieved a remarkable degree of conformity even in such matters as rising and going to sleep. They are organized strictly according to a hierarchy, the core of which is the patriarchal family. The fathers in Utopia are stern rulers over their wives and children. Women are excluded from the ranks of the decision-makers, unless they are married to a ruler. Elderly widows could occasionally become priests, which is extraordinary in the light of More's Catholicism. Women, like men, can also receive temporary military training in order to join their husbands at the front if they so wish, but only in subordinate roles. Women can also work in the fields. Their main task, however, is to look after the house, raise the children, and wait upon their husbands.

In More's time women's inferiority was mainly based on theological grounds, and even though a Christian utopia such as that of *Utopia* would strive to eliminate the original sin, the writer's impulse was to keep women thoroughly controlled in his ideal society.

---

[4]For the following discussion of More's *Utopia*, cf. Patai, "Utopia for Whom," pp. 6-7; Baruch, "A Natural and Necessary Monster," pp. 32-33.

Another important work in the line of classical utopias, Bacon's *New Atlantis* (1621), provides evidence of a further regression from the egalitarianism displayed in Plato's *Republic*.[5] The ruling forces in Bacon's plan for an ideal society are reason and science, as exemplified in the House of Salomon, the foundation of scientists, which is separated from the city of Bensalem, the center of religious and social life.[6] *New Atlantis* has justly been called a "scientific utopia."[7]

Contrary to Plato and More, Bacon does not propose a communal life-style but retains a rigidly hierarchical patriarchal family. Women are totally dominated by men and excluded from any decision-making levels, scientific endeavors or any other relevant societal processes. Not that Bacon explicitly mentions their exclusion, he simply does not mention women at all, except, that is, as housewives, the traditional role of women. Even there, however, they are to remain largely invisible. Bacon does not discuss sexuality but gives the impression that his utopia is "sexually austere and extremely conservative in its treatment of the sexes."[8]

* * *

This survey of the three most important classical utopias is not intended to suggest a linear development of the tradition. As Lyman Tower Sargent observes,

> [m]ost of the rest of the classic utopias present societies that are close to either Plato or More, with the family abolished and women fairly equal [sic], as in Campanella's *The City of the Sun* (1623), or with the family maintained and the women definitely inferior, as in Bacon's *New Atlantis* (1621).[9]

The nineteenth century saw a particular rise of utopian thinking and writing, which was, however, of a different quality than the previous mode. Elisabeth Hansot, in her study *Perfection and Progress: Two Modes of Utopian Thought*, describes the differences in thinking between classical and modern utopias.[10] She argues convincingly that classical utopias such as the ones discussed so far meant to "provide a fixed standard of judgement and an ideal in thought."[11] This accounts for their static nature. The authors were not concerned with the realization of their plan or even the possibility of its realization.[12] Applying a criterion of practicability to classical utopias in the past proved inappropriate and led to the term "utopian" assuming a derogatory connotation as "impractical, irresponsible thinking in a void."[13] According to Hansot, the classical utopia features a "primary ideal, which is addressed not to changing society but rather to measuring its worth by a fixed standard of value."[14] This standard of value was usually

---

[5]For the following discussion of *New Atlantis*, cf. Baruch, "A Natural and Necessary Monster," pp. 33-34.

[6]Hansot, *Perfection and Progress*, pp. 100-101.

[7]Baruch, "A Natural and Necessary Monster," p. 34.

[8]*ibid.*

[9]Tower Sargent, "Women in Utopia," p. 304.

[10]See n. 6.

[11]*ibid.*, p. 2.

[12]*ibid.*, p. 8.

[13]*ibid.*, p. 2.

[14]*ibid.*, p. 12.

considered absolute and universal. As "simplified, schematic construct" the author could use his utopia in order to test the implications of his ideal in a society based on its predications.[15] He did not mean to change society but he aimed rather at a change in the individual.[16]

> [t]he classical ideal corresponds to that which is thought to be most permanent and valuable in men's natures. The ideal is public, in the sense that it is capable of offering permanent satisfaction, and some men are capable of recognizing this when it is pointed out to them. The classical utopia attempts to make the reader recognize this ideal by showing him what it would be like to live in a reality determined by it and in which no complicating or contradictory factors are present.[17]

As there are always "complicating or contradictory factors" in real life, the ideal state is transcendent and ultimately unattainable. Nevertheless the standards and values are believed to exist. Consequently the classical utopia is included in the present, but remote in space, i.e. it is spatial.

> The classical utopia, located in the present, implies the real existence of the utopian ideal - the coexistence in time of the standard of judgement and that which it judges.[18]

This is perhaps best exemplified by the pun included in the name of More's fictitious island *Utopia*, a blending of the meanings "good place" (eutopia) and "no place" (outopia). Here, utopia is at once in the present and nowhere at all, i.e. it is a present ideal state which man, who is by nature limited or, in theological terms, fallen, cannot achieve.

* * *

By the time of the nineteenth century, scientists and explorers had vastly changed ways of thinking and views of the world. The end of the century was permeated by an optimistic belief in progress.

The most important change, however, seems to have been brought about by a different concept of time. Formerly, time was considered to be cyclical and the future was often expected to be simply more of the present. It was not considered to entail progressive change.[19] The idea of history as a linear, continuous and irreversible process which consequently brings about change was the immediate result of scientific discoveries in biology - notably the discovery of evolution - and geology. Both sciences opened up an immense time scale in revealing the actual geological age of the earth and the duration of evolution in comparison to the relatively short existence of *homo sapiens*.[20]

---

[15]*ibid.*, p. 19.

[16]*ibid.*, p. 13.

[17]*ibid.*, p. 17.

[18]*ibid.*, p. 95.

[19]Robert Scholes, *Structural Fabulation: An Essay on Fiction of the Future* (Notre Dame, London: University of Notre Dame Press, 1975) p. 14. Scholes discusses several concepts of time during history in this essay (pp. 12-14).

[20]Robert Scholes and Eric Rabkin, *Science Fiction: History, Science, Vision* (New York: Oxford University Press, 1977) p. 7; Hansot, *Perfection and Progress*, p. 194.

The combination of the establishment of historical thinking and the belief in progress led to a new mode of utopian thought characterized by the recognition that man can initiate social change and purposefully direct it.[21] Modern utopian thought continued the critical attitude of the classical utopia toward present reality but the idea of progressive history caused a shift from idealism to pragmatism. The modern utopian, contrary to his classical predecessor, believes in the possibility of societal change, and it is this which becomes the focus of modern utopian writing.[22] The emphasis on individual change is gone.

The new pragmatic approach analyzes problems of the present and then portrays a future in which they are overcome by an improved set of social arrangements. The modern utopia is no longer spatial but temporal.[23] It is the idea of change which is significant now: The present imperfect state becomes the past and thus provides the explanation and justification of the future utopia to which it is compared (usually through the use of a visitor from the "past", i.e. the author's present).[24] The justification of a utopian design has now become linked to the probability or possibility of its realization.[25] The pragmatism of modern utopian thinking and the new emphasis on the probability of realizing utopia is connected to the enormous rise of intentional communities in the U.S.A. since the nineteenth century.

As change becomes incorporated in modern utopian thinking and writing and as it affects a paradigm shift from the static to the dynamic, it is no longer possible to assume a fixed set of absolute values. The value system becomes both necessarily relative and subject to the ruling single ideal of the author which, in turn, is closely linked to the state of his society. Hence the relativity, as Hansot remarks:

> For the modern author, values no longer have an existence and validity independent of man: values are 'recognized' as valuable when they are seen in terms of or in contrast to the undesirable state they are designed to remedy.[26]

The social ideal is determined by present environment, not by the common nature of man.[27] Connected to this relativism is the last important paradigmatic shift from classical to modern utopia: the ideal utopian population is no longer uniform and it is not taken for granted that group interests are identical with the interests of individuals. Indeed, the more room for individual personal development and self-realization is offered, the better the utopian design.[28]

* * *

---

[21]Hansot, *Perfection and Progress*, p. 9. In the light of this distinction, Bacons's *New Atlantis* no longer appears as a purely classical utopia due to its use and purpose of science and a beginning awareness of history. It is a transitional work between the two modes. See Hansot's discussion of *New Atlantis*, pp. 99-103.

[22]*ibid.*, p. 22.

[23]*ibid.*, pp. 95, 110-111.

[24]*ibid.*, pp. 12, 15, 95, 97, 111.

[25]*ibid.*, p. 111.

[26]*ibid.*, p. 112.

[27]*ibid.*, p. 17.

[28]*ibid.*, pp. 108-109.

In accord with Hansot's thesis nineteenth century utopias show strong reformist traits and are mostly concerned with economics and education.[29]

In the chronological survey the next major model of a future society is Edward Bellamy's *Looking Backward* (1888).[30] Here, the features classified as modern utopian by Hansot can be perceived clearly when compared with the works discussed so far. For the first time in English or American literature an author placed his ideal society in the near future, the year 2000.[31] Even the place is definitely named (Boston). Robert Scholes and Eric Rabkin observe that "by bringing together a setting in the near future and a social utopian consciousness, Bellamy had created a fictional form of enormous potency."[32] His novel proved to be very influential, stimulating several counter-utopias, e.g. Morris' *News from Nowhere* (1890), which will be discussed later.

Bellamy's future society is communistic. Everybody is educated equally well and will serve for several years in the Industrial Army. Bellamy described his organization of the work-force in great detail in order to emphasize the just distribution of menial tasks and dull and heavy work. Everybody will receive a fixed number of "credits" to spend - the amount is the same for everyone and allows for decent living.

In his treatment of women Bellamy is comparatively progressive. They are freed from housework, which has been communalized (dining halls, laundries, etc.), but families live in their own houses. Women can thus pursue professional careers in their own Industrial Army which is separate from that of the men. As they are allotted their share of credits, they are economically independent of their husbands or fathers and thus much freer to take the initiative in their love lives, too. Bellamy regarded the economic dependence of women as detrimental to a good relationship between the sexes.

Despite this economic and educational equality Bellamy's future plan is deeply pervaded by the sexual polarization characteristic of the Victorian period. The sexes were not considered to be equal in the sense of identity, which was Plato's point of view. Rather, they were believed to be different but complementary. This is what enabled Bellamy, who equated female biology with weakness, still to insist on a division of labor according to sex. The following passage from *Looking Backward* exemplifies what Elaine Hoffman Baruch identifies as "male domination couched in the guise of chivalry," and Daphne Patai calls a "benevolent paternalism"[33]:

> Women being inferior in strength to men, and further disqualified industrially in special ways, the kinds of occupation reserved for them, and the conditions under which they pursue them, have reference to these facts. The heavier sorts of work are everywhere reserved for men, the lighter occupations for women. Under no circumstances is a woman permitted to follow any employment not perfectly adapted to her sex .... The men of this day so well appreciate that they owe to the beauty and grace of women the chief zest of their lives and their main incentive to effort, that they per-

---

[29]Lyman Tower Sargent, "An Ambiguous Legacy: The Role and Position of Women in the English Eutopia," in M. Barr, ed., *Future Females: A Critical Anthology* (Bowling Green, Ohio: Bowling Green State University Popular Press, 1981) p. 89.

[30]For the following discussion of *Looking Backward* cf. Baruch, "A Natural and Necessary Monster," pp. 35-37; Patai, "Utopia for Whom," pp. 7-9.

[31]Scholes and Rabkin, *Science Fiction*, p. 10.

[32]*ibid.*, p. 11.

[33]Baruch, "A Natural and Necessary Monster," p. 36; Patai, "Utopia for Whom," p. 8.

mit them to work at all only because it is fully understood that a certain regular requirement of labor, ... , is well for body and mind, during the period of maximum
physical vigor.[34]

It is obvious that women are not equal with respect to decision-making because men decide on their behalf, "permitting" them to do what they consider
suitable for them. Thus, the highest-ranking member of the women's Industrial
Army is not equal to her male counterpart: He can decide about the general ad-
ministration of the nation, whereas she only has a veto in matters concerning
women. Moreover, only married mothers are eligible for ruling posts, "as they
alone," according to Bellamy, "fully represent their sex."[35] This is reminiscent of
More's *Utopia*, although it has to be stated for fairness' sake that Bellamy tried
with serious effort and good will, to project a better world for women, too.

* * *

William Morris' *News from Nowhere* was published two years after *Looking
Backward* and is to be understood as a direct response and criticism of the latter.
Bellamy believed that technological progress was beneficient for humanity. Morris, however, seems to have been negatively impressed by the horrors of the early
Industrial Revolution and conceptualized his ideal future society as a pastoral
idyllic arcadia.[36] He renounced technology and industrialization completely. His
utopian people are artisans who take pleasure in the creativity of their work and
live simply, almost primitively. Private property does not exist, people simply take
what they need and want as there is neither money nor any substitute for it. Personal freedom for the people is a major tenet in Morris' utopia and includes sexual freedom as well. Men and women are equally free to pursue any kind of relationship they wish and they can live with whomever they want to, in large or small
groups. When a relationship is no longer wanted one can simply leave. Children
stay with the mother but are never stigmatized as illegitimate. They are always
respected. In this simple arcadia there is no institutionalized education and learning is regarded as a voluntary and life-long process.

This vision comes in the line of Plato's egalitarianism - apart from the emphasis on personal development in *News from Nowhere* - and like Plato Morris' pre-
judiced ideas about women led him to assume that once housework and child-
care are respected and honored, women would still continue engaging in these
occupations, but now happily and voluntarily. Men are considered to be inherently inept for such tasks. Morris lacked the imagination to recognize that his
basically egalitarian premises would tend to lead to new roles for both men and
women instead of reproducing the traditional ones. Although women hold a higher status in this utopia than Morris' female contemporaries did in his lifetime and
although they are depicted as physically strong, healthy, independent, as well as
participating in various kinds of work, their "natural" gravitation towards the domestic realm is characteristic of the Victorian sexual polarization.

* * *

---

[34]Edward Bellamy, *Looking Backward*, ed. Cecelia Tichi (New York: Penguin Books, 1982) p. 185.
[35]*ibid.*, p. 107.
[36]For the following discussion of *News from Nowhere*, cf. Patai, "Utopia for Whom," pp. 9-10;
Baruch, "A Natural and Necessary Monster," pp. 37-38.

19

H.G. Wells's *A Modern Utopia* (1905) refers back to Plato in several aspects.[37] Wells divided his future society into four classes according to morality, intelligence, and aptitude, thus reintroducing an elite ruling class which he called the Samurai. Work and professions are distributed among these classes according to their capabilities. In general, this future society is strictly organized and does not allow much personal freedom.

Like Plato, Wells is strongly preoccupied with eugenics. People who are allowed to procreate must meet certain physical and ecomonic standards, which excludes the lower classes. Women of the higher classes are encouraged to have eight or nine children - in fact, since Wells considered women generally inferior because they had never managed to achieve economic equality, this problem is solved in his future plan by making child-bearing and -rearing a paid profession. This is perceived to be the only way to alleviate women's economic dependence on men and to occupy them usefully since their weakness renders them unfit for any other profession. (Actually, no other opinion better illustrates male arrogance and ignorance than the notion that numerous births and the raising of many children are "light" tasks that can well be performed by "weak" women.) Consequently women do not participate in the professional public realm. In order to fulfill their procreative duties properly absolute fidelity to their husbands is required from the women by law whereas male infidelity is sanctioned. Samurai women who remain childless must either divorce or leave their class. On the other hand, lower class women who procreate without permission will be punished by the state. Except for the attempt to alleviate women's economic dependence, equality of the sexes is not a point in *A Modern Utopia*.

* * *

Baruch's statement that "utopias for men are often dystopias for women" is certainly applicable to *A Modern Utopia*.[38] The modern reader, however, may be more likely to find Wells's proposal of separate classes, breeding regulations and other restrictions rather dystopian today, anyway (although this may happen to every utopia which does not conform to the reader's own ideal). In any case the novel shares important traits with the two most famous dystopian novels in English and American literature, namely Aldous Huxley's *Brave New World* (1932) and George Orwell's *Nineteen Eighty-Four* (1949). Both of these novels are remarkable for the extensive state control of the people, either through genetic and psycho-social manipulation, as in *Brave New World*, or through all-embracing supervision and indoctrination via media and language, as in *Nineteen Eighty-Four*. It is also noteworthy that certain features such as eugenics or the dissolution of the nuclear family have been regarded as good and necessary (Plato, Mary E. Bradley Lane and modern feminist novels, e.g. *Woman on the Edge of Time*) as well as dangerous and detrimental, as in dystopian designs. This hints at the implications of the ruling ideology, which is able to use these tools for its ends. The ideology and its aims ultimately outweigh the question of technology and its uses. Also, the views of ideology and the related use of technology in utopian and dystopian writing throw a light on the author's own value system and political priorities. Huxley, Orwell and other contemporary authors of dystopian literature no longer shared the optimism regarding technological progress espoused by Bel-

---

[37]For the following discussion, cf. Patai, "Utopia for Whom," pp. 10-13; Annette Keinhorst, *Utopien von Frauen in der zeitgenössischen Literatur der U.S.A.* (Frankfurt *et al.*: Peter Lang, 1985) pp. 8-9.
[38]Baruch, "A Natural and Necessary Monster," p. 38.

lamy and Wells. The two world wars and the negative side-effects of industrialization and technology as well as the disastrous experience of totalitarian states
did not serve to further utopian optimism about the future; rather they
contributed to shifting the emphasis to warning about possible disastrous future
effects of certain aspects of present-day society. This new direction and the increase in dystopian writing marked an important cut in the literary utopian tradition.

* * *

As Tower Sargent observes, "the contemporary utopia is found almost exclusively in science fiction."[39] This genre with narrative devices such as interstellar
travel, alien encounters and time travel possesses an enormous variety of means
to describe alternative societies; this has not, however, been the major concern of
science fiction because it has been influenced by other literary genres and societal developments. The variety of future conceptions and societies in science fiction constitutes enough material for another study, but they cannot for the most
part be regarded as belonging to a truly utopian tradition.

Let me therefore conclude my survey of modern utopias by mentioning the
growing coherence and inclusiveness of the depicted conceptions of the future.
The authors not only created different social organizations which were to be better than their own; they also explored the consequences of these organizations
for other cultural aspects. An example is Bellamy's description of artistic activity
in *Looking Backward*, which mirrors the principles he has set up for his social
ideal of economic equality.[40] Such an ideal will determine all activities in a utopia, not only the social ones.[41]

Wells, unlike Plato, included a description of the lives of the lower classes in
his *A Modern Utopia*.

Nevertheless, modern utopias seem not to be able to maintain the dynamic
element of change that brings them into existence. In the end, they seem to be as
static as their classical forerunners because, as they presumably have achieved
perfection already, there is no incentive left for further change.[42]

From Plato onwards the development of utopian societies has become more
and more firmly established in fiction as a means to express the author's values
and/or social ideals and to test them in a speculative thought-experiment. But,
again since Plato, the utopian mode of thinking has been connected to philosophical and political thinking as a mode of argumentation or persuasion in meta-
phorical or analogical form (e.g. Marxism/socialism, feminism). Utopian writing
has never been pursued solely as "art for art's sake," or for purely aesthetical pur-
poses, it has always implied a critique of existing societies. It is a well-known
truism that a utopia often reveals more about its author and his or her own time
than about the future.[43] Literary criticism should always be aware of this.

---

[39]Tower Sargent, "Women in Utopia," p. 308.

[40]Hansot, *Perfection and Progress*, pp. 14-15.

[41]*ibid.*, pp. 20, 112.

[42]*ibid.*, p. 98.

[43]This is the reason why I have assumed that the ideas and ideals expressed in utopian writing are
identical with those of the author. I am aware of the fact that this sort of equation of work and
author is generally not permitted in literary criticism. Nevertheless, I consider it justified in the case
of this genre for the reasons stated here.

1.2 The Genres: Utopia, Science Fiction, Fantasy - An Explication of Terminology

The transference of utopia into contemporary science fiction, mainly caused by the development of the near-future modern utopia on the one hand and the impact of science and technology on the other, resulted in a partial merging of genres that has led to problems in the area of classification. Clearly, most of science fiction has nothing to do with the utopian tradition at all. If, however, a fictional model of society is built extensively on science and technology, is it still a utopia or is it science fiction? Bellamy's *Looking Backward*, for instance, is often listed in the ancestry of science fiction.[44]

The boundaries between science fiction and fantasy are even more blurred. Often critics use these terms in different ways and they do not always clarify them. In what follows I shall delineate how I intend to use the terms utopia, science fiction, and fantasy.

* * *

In the use of the term *utopia* as a genre I have followed Hansot's requirement that a utopia "would have to describe all the major social arrangements an author thinks necessary and desirable for the good life."[45] The fictitious society needs to be wholly and coherently described, it is not enough to alter only a few institutions. As an antonym I shall use *dystopia*.

Several distinctions can be drawn within the genre. I have already discussed classical and modern, spatial and temporal utopias.

A temporal utopia can be *future oriented* and thus coincide partially with science fiction. Science and technology will be integrated for the good of humanity (e.g. Bellamy's *Looking Backward*). A *past oriented* utopia usually displays an anti-technological attitude and would revert to the simple life-style of former times which is believed to be better (e.g. Morris' *News from Nowhere*). This subgenre can be related to the pastoral which in turn refers to the lost mythical Golden Age.[46]

Modern utopias from the 1970s onward which are written by politically committed authors with the intention of educating their readers and inciting them to respond emotionally to a different way of life, and to take an interest in politics, are often called *social utopias*.[47]

* * *

The term *critical utopia*, introduced by Tom Moylan, refers to fictitious utopian societies "related to and in conflict with nonutopian, parent societies" which exist simultaneously.[48] This sub-genre is thus related to the sociological and pol-

---

[44]See for example Scholes and Rabkin, *Science Fiction*, pp. 6, 10-11.

[45]Hansot, *Perfection and Progress*, p. 3.

[46]For a more elaborate discussion of future and past oriented utopias, their origin and developments and their political, theological, and philosophical implications see Heide Göttner-Abendroth, "Der unversöhnliche Traum - Utopie in der Neuen Linken und in der Frauenbewegung," *Ästhetik und Kommunikation*, 10,37 (October 1979) pp. 5-15.

[47]Keinhorst, *Utopien von Frauen*, pp. 15-16.

[48]Tom Moylan, "Beyond Negation: The Critical Utopias of Ursula K. LeGuin and Samuel R. Delany," *Extrapolation*, 21,3 (1980) p. 237. Cf. Keinhorst's *Utopien von Frauen*, pp. 15-16.

itical "concrete utopia", which is not a literary term but refers to actual utopian experiments - often in communes - in a historical non-utopian society or to a theoretical regulative idea intended to serve as instruction to political action.[49]

A critical utopia is not, however, considered to belong to the utopian genre but to science fiction.[50] Here it is obvious how confusing the use of terminology has become due to undifferentiated usage, but also because of the increasing congruence of the utopian tradition and that pole of science fiction which is concerned with alternative utopian societies. These could, in science fiction, be presented as parallel worlds in alternate universes (e.g. Joanna Russ, *The Female Man*, 1975) or as colonies or societies of aliens on another planet (e.g. Theodore Sturgeon, *Venus Plus X*, 1960). The non-utopian parent societies, however, are not necessarily the societies of the authors but are often future projections, too, especially those societies which can use interstellar travel and visit or colonize other planets. This mainly places the critical utopia in a science fiction frame.

* * *

Science fiction is a comparatively young literary genre which can draw on a wide variety of older literary traditions. Darko Suvin lists the following:

> the Greek and Hellenistic "blessed island" stories, the "fabulous voyage" from Antiquity on, the Renaissance and Baroque "utopia" and "planetary novel", the Enlightenment "state (political) novel", the modern "anticipation", "anti-utopia" etc.[51]

As mentioned above, the utopian tradition is also regarded as a predecessor. Moreover, certain similarities can be found to fairy tales, myths, sagas, pastoral, and fantasy.[52]

In spite of the wealth of such ancestry and association, critics generally agree that the actual starting-point of the genre is Mary Shelley's Gothic horror story *Frankenstein* (1818).[53] In this romanticist novel, science and its dangers are the central themes, but not with regard to society. For a long time science fiction remained speculative on the future development of technology (e.g. Jules Verne). This direction, which came to dominate the American pulp "fanzines" for years, is called "hardware" or "hard" science fiction, because of its orientation towards "hard" sciences (astronomy, physics, biology, biochemistry).[54] Several authors of this direction were engineers (e.g. Robert Heinlein) or scientists (e.g. Arthur C. Clarke, Isaac Asimov).[55]

At the end of the 1950s and throughout the 1960s science fiction writers began to take an increasing interest in the "soft" sciences such ethology, ecology, psy-

---

[49]See Moylan, "Beyond Negation," p. 237; Göttner-Abendroth, "Der unversöhnlich Traum," p. 7.

[50]See Moylan, "Beyond Negation," p. 236.

[51]Darko Suvin, "On the Poetics of the Science Fiction Genre," *College English*, 34,3 (1972) p. 372. Cf. also Mark R. Hillegas, "The Literary Background to Science Fiction," in *Science Fiction - A Critical Guide*, P. Parrinder, ed. (London, New York: Longman, 1979) pp. 2-17, for an elaborate representation.

[52]Suvin, "On the Poetics of the Science Fiction Genre," p. 372; Scholes and Rabkin, *Science Fiction*, pp. 6-7.

[53]For example, see Scholes and Rabkin, *Science Fiction*, p. 6; Keinhorst, *Utopien von Frauen*, p. 12.

[54]Scholes and Rabkin, *Science Fiction*, p. 12; Joanna Russ, "The Image of Women in Science Fiction," *Red Clay Reader*, 7 (1970) p. 35.

[55]Scholes and Rabkin, *Science Fiction*, pp. 55, 58, 65.

chology and even para-psychology.[56] "Soft" science fiction deals with social issues and institutions. The precursor of this direction is H.G. Wells with his concept of "social engineering".[57]

Within the scope of this study it is impossible to further delineate the evolution of science fiction as a literary genre. Its development is well documented.[58] Nevertheless, definitions and boundaries are often left blurred. This is partly caused by the amount of badly written formula science fiction which often does not fit any genre at all but confuses the general notion as to what science fiction is.[59] Joanna Russ calls science fiction "*What If*-literature" because it

> shows things not as they characteristically are but as they might be, and for this "might be" the author must offer a rational, serious, consistent explanation, one that does not (in Samuel Delany's phrase) offend against what is known to be known.[60]

Darko Suvin went beyond this concise definition and tried to outline science fiction as a coherent and distinct genre. In his important essay "On the Poetics of the Science Fiction Genre" he defined science fiction as the "literature of cognitive estrangement."[61]

> SF is, then a literary genre whose necessary and sufficient conditions are the presence and interaction of estrangement and cognition, and whose main formal device is an imaginative framework alternative to the author's empirical environment.[62]

This points beyond a mere agreement on the necessity to treat future marvels in a rational, logical, and detailed manner. In the light of this definition, Suvin sees science fiction as a thought-provoking and educational genre, which should discuss the uses and effects of sciences.[63]

He distinguishes two major models of science fiction. The *extrapolative* model is oriented futurologically. As in a scientific experiment, it poses one or several hypotheses which are deduced from the present and then consistently developed to a logical end.[64] This is also known as the "scientific method" of science fiction.[65]

The *analogic* model insists much less on empiricism. Suvin states that

---

[56]Russ, "The Image of Women in Science Fiction," p. 35. For a very good survey of science fiction, its relation to scientific development in its evolution as a literary genre, see Scholes and Rabkin, *Science Fiction*.

[57]Scholes and Rabkin, *Science Fiction*, pp. 14-25.

[58]Scholes and Rabkin, *Science Fiction*, are one example. See the bibliography therein.

[59]One example is the "Space Opera" which transposes the pattern of a Western into space. The same pattern, but peopled with knights and ladies instead, is called "Sword and Sorcery". Both are not considered science fiction. See Scholes and Rabkin, *Science Fiction*, pp. 171-172.

[60]Joanna Russ, "'What If . . . ?' Literature," in *The Contemporary Literary Scene 1973*, F.V. Magill, ed. (Englewood Cliffs, N.J.: Salem Press, 1974) p. 197.

[61]Suvin, "On the Poetics of the Science Fiction Genre," p. 378.

[62]*ibid.*, p. 375.

[63]*ibid.*, p. 381.

[64]*ibid.*, pp. 378-379.

[65]See, for instance, Pamela Annas, "New Worlds, New Words: Androgyny in Feminist Science Fiction," *Science Fiction Studies*, 5 (1978) p. 143.

24

[t]he objects, figures, and up to a point the relationships from which this indirectly modelled world starts can be quite fantastic (in the sense of empirically unverifiable) as long as they are logically, philosophically and mutually consistent.[66]

I shall adhere in the following to Russ's and Suvin's definitions of science fiction as mostly future-oriented literature whose central theme is science in order to explain the phenomena it describes coherently and logically, as if they were true.

* * *

Suvin's analogic model which allows for a fantastic setting borders on fantasy. The distinction between these two genres often seems to be difficult because they both postulate conditions which do not exist in the author's empirically known world. Scholes's and Rabkin's suggestion that science fiction could be defined by its elements and fantasy by its structure is not really helpful, however.[67] Good science fiction aims at plausibility and coherence of its postulations, even the hypothetical and speculative ones have a relation to the known world. Fantasy, on the other hand, is distinct from science fiction and utopia because of its use of supernatural miracles of nature and improbable developments in all possible areas as metaphors and allegories. The empirical environment is deliberately interspersed with anti-cognitive laws. Fantasy is close to the fairy tale and to myth and it also appears as the ghost, horror, Gothic, or weird tale.[68]

The boundaries between literary genres are never absolutely sharp, and here they are particularly fluid. There are always literary works that do not fit neatly into categories. One should keep in mind that this is often the case with utopias, science fiction, and fantasy.

1.3 Women Writers and the Use of the Utopian Tradition

Women writing in English have written extensively within the utopian tradition. Daphne Patai listed one hundred and two items of utopian writing by women in an - as yet incomplete - bibliography. She found that most of them contain two different ideological clusters. One in its extreme form includes a variable mix of traditional gender roles, militarism, chauvinism, racism, anti-communism, and anti-feminism. Opposed to this is a cluster which contains pacifism, egalitarianism, socialism , and feminism.[69] In accord with this study, the following survey will only consider the latter type.

* * *

In 1762 Sarah Robinson Scott published *A Description of Millenium Hall, and the Country Adjacent.* This semi-autobiographical novel features an all-women society living in the English countryside. It does not qualify as a utopian novel according to my definition of utopia because it does not include different institutions or social arrangements on a societal plane. But *Millenium Hall* is

---

[66]Suvin, "On the Poetics of the Science Fiction Genre," p. 379.

[67]Scholes and Rabkin, *Science Fiction*, p. 170.

[68]Suvin, "On the Poetics of the Science Fiction Genre," p. 375.

[69]Daphne Patai, "British and American Utopias by Women (1836-1979): An Annotated Bibliography, Part I," *Alternative Futures*, 4, 2/3 (1981) pp. 184-206, 186.

concerned with an alternative way of female life in terms of the Christian virtues of piety, chastity, and charity. The women despise selfishness and the accumulation of wealth. They also emphasize the importance of a good and classical education for women which is modelled on the kind of education given to contemporary noblewomen. As Jane Spencer points out in her introduction to *Millenium Hall* this novel is not only written with a didactic intention for young women, it is also directed at men. Sarah Scott intended her women to be perfect models of benevolence who should influence men and induce them to follow their example.[70] Despite the utopian vision of a caring female community, however, Sarah Scott is not concerned with the abolition of class barriers and she does not question woman's subordinate status in marriage.

* * *

In the following century the American Elizabeth Stuart Phelps wrote three utopian fantasies which concerned the heavenly afterlife.[71] They do not therefore belong to the truly utopian tradition which deals with ideal human societies on earth. Nevertheless they are noteworthy in this context because of their feminist themes: Phelps calls for reformed fathers and husbands who are required to participate in housekeeping and child-rearing so that the women are also able to pursue their own needs. Carol Farley Kessler comments that Phelps believed the Christian religion offered women the equality which the politics of their time denied them.[72] The placement of utopia in the afterlife, however, does not evidence any optimism with regard to women's situation in their actual lives. Female utopian writers are usually concerned with envisioning better *living* conditions for women.

* * *

Mary E. Bradley Lane's novel *Mizora: A Prophecy*, which first appeared in serialized form from 1880 to 1881, features an all-women society located in the interior of the earth. The men have all disappeared presumably after a war of the sexes. The women no longer needed them since they had developed parthenogenesis. Sex is not discussed apart from the implication that it formerly (i.e. when the men were still there) degraded women.

The disappearance of men brought about a superior civilization with remarkable achievements in technology. Most important, however, is the association of men with violence, which has disappeared along with them.[73] Security precautions and laws are not needed in *Mizora*. This has since become a paradigm in all-women utopias.

From a modern feminist point of view *Mizora*, however, is not flawless. It still includes a class system and servants and also features eugenics which has led to a uniformly blond and blue-eyed white race of women.

---

[70]Jane Spencer, Introd. *Millenium Hall*, by Sarah Robinson Scott (London: Virago, 1986) pp. xi, xv.
[71]Elizabeth Stuart Phelps, *The Gates Ajar* (1868), *Beyond the Gates* (1883), *The Gates Between* (1887). See Carol Farley Kessler, "The Heavenly Utopia of Elizabeth Stuart Phelps," in *Women and Utopia - Critical Interpretations*, Barr and Smith, eds. (Lanham *et al.*: University Press of America, 1983) pp. 85-95.
[72]Kessler, "The Heavenly Utopia of Elizabeth Stuart Phelps," pp. 87-88.
[73]Cf. Patai, "British and American Utopias by Women," p. 189-190; Keinhorst, *Utopien von Frauen*, pp. 121-124.

Mrs. George Corbett's *New Amazonia: A Foretaste of the Future* (1889) is set in the Ireland of 2472.[74] Only women are eligible for ruling posts, and they have to be unmarried. This is in direct opposition to Bellamy's mother cult in *Looking Backward*. Otherwise the sexes are treated equally. Marriage and divorce are easy. Every woman is allowed to have only four children, which are maintained by the state until they are twenty and are all given a good and equal education. The state in general controls most aspects of life. Eugenics and euthanasia are practiced - these often accompany utopias and dystopias which feature state control.

* * *

Unveiling a Parallel: A Romance (1893), written under a pseudonym by Alice Ilgenfritz Jones and Ella Merchant, compares three different societies.[75] One of them is the authors' society on Earth. The other two imaginary societies are situated on Mars. Women are equal to men in both. In one of them, however, women have become like men in a negative way, i.e. they share such "vices" as going to brothels and the like. In the other Martian societiy both sexes share a utopian life and are kind, loving, and generous. Obviously, the authors share Plato's point of view that men and women do not have different natures but are essentially alike, both equally capable of good and evil.

* * *

This point of view was not shared by Charlotte Perkins Gilman, who wrote the best known precursor to contemporary feminist utopian writing, namely *Herland*, which appeared in serialized form in her own feminist magazine *The Forerunner* in 1915.[76] Gilman is associated with nineteenth century Cultural Feminism, which maintained that women should collectively and separately (i.e. apart from men) make an effort to discover their real nature which is different from men's as well as different from what men had up to then considered woman's nature.[77] This stream of feminism affirmed and emphasized what it perceived to be essentially feminine qualities, such as pacifism, cooperation, dislike of violence and a harmonious form of government. Cultural Feminism went beyond the more reformist demands of Liberal Feminism in the tradition of Mary Wollstonecraft and aimed at a more radical cultural transformation according to the above mentioned feminine qualities, which included questioning the value of institutions which had hitherto not been subjected to questioning, such as religion, marriage and the nuclear family, as well as the imagination and proposal of possible alternatives. It is the immediate precursor of today's Radical Feminism.

---

[74]Cf. also Patai, "British and American Utopias by Women," p. 189; Tower Sargent, "Women in Utopia," pp. 306-307.

[75]Patai, "British and American Utopias by Women," p. 191.

[76]*ibid.*, p. 193.

[77]For this outline of Cultural Feminism see Josephine Donovan, *Feminist Theory: The Intellectual Traditions of American Feminism* (New York: Ungar, 1985) chap. 2, pp. 31-63. This chapter includes a discussion of Gilman's oeuvre.

Gilman's matriarchal all-women society of *Herland* exemplifies the postulates of Cultural Feminism in fiction. A geographical catastrophe had bereaved it of most of its men and isolated it from the rest of the world. The women, after having slain the few remaining men who attempted to oppress them, miraculously developed parthenogenesis and created a complex culture and civilization superior to the outer world. The women are cooperative and peaceful. As in *Mizora*, the absence of violence is the consequence of the absence of men and the possibility of free movement for women is repeatedly emphasized.

Due to the geographically determined necessity of restricting overpopulation the women are each allowed to bear one child only. Exceptionally bright women are allowed to have more children and to become "over-mothers", whereas women who are considered morally inferior are not allowed to have children. This eugenically inspired regulation, which is slightly reminiscent of Wells's *A Modern Utopia*, is reflected in the complete control of nature: Plants and animals which were considered useless have simply been exterminated. This is also in accord with the Social Darwinism of Gilman's time. Such an attitude towards nature and the strong mother cult of *Herland* do not seem desirable to feminists today.

Like Lane and Bellamy, whose socialist ideas appealed strongly to her, Gilman believed in a beneficient outcome of technology for humanity. However, much of the description of *Herland* reveals it as a pastoral where life is simple. There are no laws - these are no longer necessary since violence has disappeared along with the men - nor are there any institutions. As in Morris' *News from Nowhere* children are not schooled but educated in nurseries in a playful way by specially trained women. Learning is again a life-long and voluntary process, but the women have high standards and demand the best of every member.

In the sequel "With Her in Ourland", serialized in *The Forerunner* one year later, in 1916, this superior women's world is contrasted to Gilman's own society and constitutes a social critique of its ills.

* * *

During the last twenty years utopian writing by women, in the context of science fiction, increased so enormously that it is impossible to outline it further. I shall refer to various works in this tradition in connection with the three novels which will be discussed in the next section.

Let me conclude this survey with a few general observations. I have previously mentioned the difficulty in classifying literary works according to the genres utopia, science fiction, and fantasy. Utopian writing by women seems to be even more elusive and less suited to these categories. As stated above, Sarah Scott's *Millenium Hall* and Elizabeth Stuart Phelps's novels do not qualify as utopias in any sense of the genre definition proposed here. Nevertheless, utopian elements are strongly represented. Scott's tentative use of a utopian conception has the character of an entreating appeal to male rationality in order to make men realize that women are able and efficient.

Phelps's afterlife utopias evidence strong criticism of gender roles. She literally does not see any hope for a better life for women on earth, however, and offers consolation in religion instead.

Unveiling a Parallel expresses the opinion that all people are equal in their nature regardless of their sex. The depiction of the utopian society does not necessarily lead to the conclusion that the authors considered it ideal, it may at best be seen as the expression of the conviction that both sexes can set up a virtuous society as well as an evil one.

Corbett's *New Amazonia* offers only a "rather odd mixture of reforms" which are rather incoherent and cannot be traced to a single ruling ideal.[78]

The two feminist utopias, *Mizora* and *Herland*, are spatial like the classical utopias. This leads to the conclusion that the authors did not consider their utopias to be realizable, unlike e.g. Bellamy, who saw the Boston of the future as inherent in the Boston he saw around him. Nor did Gilman and Lane explore universal values as did their classical precursors. Rather they used their all-women societies to demonstrate that, without male interference and when their potential is fully realized, women are equal to men. The choice of a spatial utopia, which exists at the same time as the author's society, underlines the opinion that women *are already equal*, and it is men who suppress their potential. Although Cultural Feminism promoted separatism in order for women to be able to define their true nature, it did not propagate unisex societies. Despite their extensive depiction, Gilman's and Lane's utopias are not meant as blueprints. Like *Unveiling a Parallel*, they are symbolic in character, but politically strongly motivated, thus having a more overt didactic purpose.

Utopian writing by women had come a long way from the pleading character of Scott's *Millenium Hall* to a thorough statement of women's equality in Gilman's *Herland*. It still remained for later feminist writers to create alternative societies and propose them as future models.

---

[78]Tower Sargent, "Women in Utopia," p. 307.

2. DISCUSSION OF THE NOVELS

In this section I shall discuss three novels by contemporary women writers who designed alternative societies which imply comments on the situation of women in our present society and which contain utopian elements with respect to women.

In the case of Ursula K. LeGuin's *The Left Hand of Darkness*, a utopia is not intended but the implications and consequences of the depicted hermaphroditic/androgynous society constitute a critique of the situation of women in our culture and argue that the basic psychological equality of the sexes should be realized.

Marge Piercy's *Woman on the Edge of Time* is not so much metaphorically but rather practically oriented. Her future society is meant to be a model of how both men and women could live together harmoniously once they have been able to recognize and eliminate our present destructive gender roles.

The Wanderground by Sally Miller Gearhart is an example of an all-women society as could be favored by contemporary Lesbian Separatism. She deals most strongly with what she perceives to be male and female qualities and is most pessimistic about the possibility of a near-future synthesis into androgyny.

The choice of these three novels as examples of the large variety that women writers' novels about better alternative worlds evidence neither intends to present them as prototypes of this variety - which is far richer - nor does it suggest a linear development (i.e. from abstract thought-experiments to separatist women's cultures).

The different societies created in these novels offer the opportunity to look at the connections between the form of the imagined society and certain feminist theories, and how the interplay between these determines form, structure, narrative devices, and imagery.

2.1 Ursula K. LeGuin: *The Left Hand of Darkness*

Ursula K. LeGuin's novel *The Left Hand of Darkness* was published in 1969, at about the time the New Feminism was beginning to impart strength to the Women's Movement, which had lost much of its impact on U.S. society through the early decades of this century. In her article "Is Gender Necessary?" LeGuin attempted to describe how, having previously considered herself a feminist in the tradition of Emmeline Pankhurst and Virginia Woolf, this "groundswell gathering" of the Women's Movement, influenced her novel:[1]

---

[1]Ursula K. LeGuin, "Is Gender Necessary?" in *The Language of the Night*, Susan Wood, ed. (New York: G.B. Putnam's Sons, 1979) p. 161. This essay was first published in 1976 in *Aurora: Beyond Equality*, V.N. McIntyre, S.J. Anderson, eds. (Greenwich, CT: Fawcett, 1976).

Along about 1967, I began to feel a certain unease, a need to step on a little farther, perhaps, on my own. I began to want to define and understand the meaning of sexuality and the meaning of gender, in my life and in our society. Much had gathered in the unconscious - both personal and collective - which must either be brought up into consciousness, or else turn destructive. It was that same need, I think, that had led Beauvoir to write *The Second Sex*, . . . But I was not a theoretician, a political thinker or activist, or sociologist. I was and am a fiction writer. The way I did my thinking was to write a novel. That novel, *The Left Hand of Darkness*, is the record of my consciousness, the process of my thinking.[2]

Ursula K. LeGuin, who had read science fiction extensively in her youth, later rediscovered this genre in the early sixties. She found out that it had by then been much improved and was being used by accomplished writers.[3] She started to write science fiction short stories and sold some to science fiction and fantasy magazines. Before writing *The Left Hand of Darkness*, LeGuin had published three novels, each of which constitutes a mix of science fiction and fantasy with a tendency, however, towards the latter with their use of elvish creatures, winged cats, fairy tale settings and of the quest journey for (often a lost) identity.[4] These novels aim at the average science fiction and fantasy reader without any pretensions to high art - LeGuin herself regards them as her apprenticeship in the realm of science fiction and fantasy and as rather incomplete.[5] They do introduce, however, some of the recurrent themes or her oeuvre, such as loyalty, trust, human friendship, and a sense of moral obligation. Moreover, they already establish LeGuin's "Hainish" universe, in which human life is brought to all inhabitable planets of the universe, including the Earth, by the people of the planet Hain. This fact enables her to describe different worlds in different novels which refer to each other but do not constitute sequels. As each world is ruled by its own special conditions, the universe offers enough "humans" to "display enough variety to provide for any number of alien encounters, . . ., new definitions of 'civilization' can be made in a narrative rather than in a discursive mode."[6] The use of a single, historically continuous universe in a writer's oeuvre is a common device of science fiction and not original to LeGuin.[7]

* * *

The Left Hand of Darkness is LeGuin's first authentic science fiction novel and it was her first major success. It won both the Nebula and Hugo Awards in 1970.[8]

---

[2]*ibid.*, pp. 161-162.

[3]Ursula K. LeGuin, "A Citizen of Mondath," in *The Language of the Night*, pp. 25-30. This article originally appeared in *Foundation*, 4 (1973).

[4]*Rocannon's World* (1966), *Planet of Exile* (1966), *City of Illusions* (1967).

[5]LeGuin, "A Citizen of Mondath," pp. 28-29; Interview with Paul Walker, *Luna Monthly*, 63 (March 1976) pp. 1-7.

[6]Douglas Barbour, "Wholeness and Balance in the Hainish Novels of Ursula K. LeGuin," *Science Fiction Studies*, 1,3 (1974) p. 164.

[7]Carol McGuirk, "Optimism and the Limits of Subversion in *The Dispossessed* and *The Left Hand of Darkness*," in *Ursula K. LeGuin*, H. Bloom, ed. (New York *et al.*: Chelsea House Publishers, 1984) p. 249.

[8]The Nebula Award is granted by the members of the Science Fiction Writers of America. The Hugo Award is granted by fans at the World Science Fiction Convention. See Scholes and Rabkin, *Science Fiction*, pp. 242-243.

Moreover, LeGuin received the attention of a wider critical and academic audience after Robert Scholes's article "The Good Witch of the West" in 1975 - indeed, the criticism of her works is extraordinarily extensive for a writer of science fiction and fantasy.[9]

In *The Left Hand of Darkness*, set in the distant future of LeGuin's Hainish cosmos, most of the worlds which are inhabited by human life are joined together into the Ekumen. This organisation is not a political unit in the sense of an empire, but "a co-ordinator, a clearing house for trade and knowledge."[10] The action of the novel takes place on a planet which is not yet a member of the Ekumen and as its people have not developed any means of interstellar communication or travel, they do not even know about other planets inhabited by human beings.

This planet was given the name Winter because of its harsh glacial climate by the investigators of the Ekumen who went there unrecognized in order to evaluate the developmental stage of humanoid life. The hermaphroditic native inhabitants call it Gethen. In order to inform the Gethenians about the Ekumen and to invite them to join, the Ekumen has sent a First Mobile whose task is to give evidence of the Ekumen and explain its policies and possibilities. This messenger, Genly Ai from Earth, comes alone in order to show that the Ekumen does not want to force or conquer, but only to make an offer. Genly Ai, described by LeGuin herself as a "conventional, rather stuffy, young man,"[11] in his early thirties, lands in Karhide, one of Gethen's two large nations. This nation somewhat resembles a feudal monarchy with loosely structured and largely independent Domains. Genly's cause is supported by Therem Harth rem ir Estraven, who is introduced as a powerful politician and intimate of the king of Karhide but who loses the king's favor and is exiled very early in the novel. Genly is used as a pawn in this intrigue against Estraven but fails to comprehend it. He cannot convince the king to make contact with the Ekumen and eventually, when the intrigue makes life in Karhide dangerous for him, he leaves for the other large nation on Gethen, Orgoreyn.This nation is modelled on a modern bureaucracy with a profit-oriented economy and considerable state control of its citizens. Again, Genly is caught between two rival political factions and sacrificed to their goals. His lack of understanding the foreign policies and his mistrust of Estraven, the only person on the whole planet who believes in him and is dedicated to his cause, make him end up in an Orgota work camp where he would have died of cold and an alien medication which does not match his physiology, if Estraven had not rescued him. Much of Genly Ai's mistrust and lack of understanding is rooted in his confusion about the peculiar Gethenian hermaphroditic physiology and its implications, but he begins to trust Estraven and to understand the complex reasons and intrigues that caused the failure of his mission so far. Estraven leads Genly back to Karhide in a daring, arduous, and seemingly impossible trek across a huge glacier, the Gobrin Ice. Shortly after their arrival in Karhide Estraven is killed upon the command of his rival and successor, but as he had managed

---

[9]Robert Scholes, "The Good Witch of the West," *Structural Fabulation*, pp. 77-99. For bibliographies of criticism on LeGuin see Jeff Levin, "Ursula K. LeGuin: A Select Bibliography," *Science Fiction Studies*, 2,3 (1975) pp. 204-208; "Bibliographic Checklist of the Works of Ursula K. LeGuin," in *The Language of the Night*, pp. 237-270; Marshall B. Tymn, "Ursula K. LeGuin: A Bibliography," in *Ursula K. LeGuin*, Olander and Greenberg, eds. (New York: Taplinger Publishing Company, 1979) pp. 241-246. See also Keinhorst, *Utopien von Frauen*, pp. 22-24.

[10]Ursula K. LeGuin, *The Left Hand of Darkness* (New York: Harper & Row Publishers, 1969) p. 24. Subsequent references to this edition will be placed within the text in parentheses.

[11]LeGuin, "Is Gender Necessary?" p. 163.

to send a message to the king of Karhide which will make him accept Genly's mission, his rival himself loses favor again and Genly is finally able to complete his mission and summon his colleagues who had waited in a starship in orbit around Gethen's sun.

* * *

This rough outline of *The Left Hand of Darkness* shows that it is a science fiction novel according to Suvin's analogic model. The setting on the planet Winter/Gethen is somewhat fantastic since its glacial epoch does not constitute an extrapolation of our known world. This is even less the case with its biologically unique inhabitants. LeGuin, however, took great pains in creating a logically coherent world. Thus, the glacial epoch, its seasons, climate, and meteorological peculiarities are scientifically explained by an elliptoid orbit, the planet's tilt, and meteorological laws of air currents which are all based on empirical science (*The Left Hand of Darkness*, p. 147, pp. 149-150).[12] Even more care is given to the ethnographic description of the Gethenians. LeGuin's Gethenians possess both male and female reproductive organs and are subject to an oestrous cycle which renders them sexually inactive and impotent for most of the time. Once a month they enter a phase of sexual capability called *kemmer*. They then become either male or female - their sex may change every month arbitrarily. LeGuin devoted a whole chapter to the discussion of Gethenian hermaphroditism in the form of anthropological field notes taken by an investigator who preceded Genly Ai (*The Left Hand of Darkness*, chap. 7).[13] The relationship to empirical biology is obvious and the scientific coherence of Gethenian physiology, including Karhidish special terminology, is all-encompassing.

* * *

The most important science used as background to *The Left Hand of Darkness*, however, is anthropology. LeGuin, the daughter of the renowned anthropologist Alfred L. Kroeber, whose major corpus deals with American Indians, draws a vivid and authentic picture of the Gethenians' social life with the help of mythical tales and sagas. These explain ethic mores, moral traditions, religious beliefs, and related attitudes. Even a creation myth is included which takes account of the ice age, the hermaphroditic physiology, and the fact that the Gethenian humans are the only mammals of their planet. Throughout the whole novel the reader is confronted with a people of a different mentality which is in accord with their living conditions. I shall at present only mention the absence of the emphasis on technological and economic progress in a glacial world which allows only slow motion, and the special way of asserting personal prestige (shifgrethor), which cannot be connected to stereotypical sex-role behavior. In the special discussions of particular societal aspects in section 3 I shall point out how LeGuin was influenced by her knowledge of American Indian and Chinese cultures.

---

[12]Cf. also LeGuin's opinion that scientific knowledge is necessary in order to write good science fiction and to channel the science fiction writer's imagination in her essay "Do-it-Yourself Cosmology," in *The Language of the Night*, pp. 121-125. This essay was first published in *Parabola*, 2,3 (1977).
[13]Cf. Frank Robert Vivelo, *Cultural Anthropology Handbook: A Basic Introduction* (New York et al.: McGraw-Hill Book Company, 1978) Part I, for a description of anthropological methods. See esp. pp. 9-10 on field notes.

The author's use of science is in accord with the genre definition of science fiction proposed here. Both the extrapolative and the analogic model of science fiction constitute a commentary on the present empirical world and its sciences. Extrapolation in science fiction is more future-oriented that analogy because it is concerned with the future development of a particular science and its possible future effects. The prospect can be pessimistic as well as optimistic but refers back to the present situation. According to Suvin's idea of science fiction as an educational genre this should stimulate discussion about the sciences in question. LeGuin herself rejects this model and its predictive character. In the introduction to *The Left Hand of Darkness* she states:

> Strictly extrapolative works of science fiction generally arrive about where the Club of Rome arrives: somewhere between the gradual extinction of human liberty and the total extinction of terrestrial life .... Almost anything carried to its logical extreme becomes depressing, if not carcinogenic. (*The Left Hand of Darkness*, vii)

LeGuin therefore prefers the analogic mode which she regards as a more comprehensive thought-experiment than the narrower focus of extrapolation would allow. The analogical model does not concentrate on one science but requires the creation of an alternative society analogous to our own, either set in the distant future or on a different planet. Despite the future setting, however, this model is strongly oriented towards the present. LeGuin maintains that "the future, in fiction, is a metaphor," (*The Left Hand of Darkness*, x) and that a science fiction thought-experiment should describe "reality, the present world" (*The Left Hand of Darkness*, viii).

Analogic science fiction describes rather than prescribes. The analogic alternative world is a direct commentary on our own.

All of this applies to *The Left Hand of Darkness*. The use of a different world with different people, a different value system and so on constitutes the essence of Suvin's idea of cognitive estrangement. On the one hand, Gethen is different from our world due to its ice age, but it is not entirely alien. Similarly, the Gethenians are aliens, but at the same time they are recognizably human. Thus estrangement and cognition interact as simultaneous responses of the reader and incites her/him to look at Gethen as if it were a mirror of the Earth. Suvin required that science fiction "not ask about the Man or the World, but which man?: in which kind of world?: and why such a man in such a kind of world?"[14] *The Left Hand of Darkness* as a thought-experiment poses exactly these questions. Gethen is not a utopia because Earth at present is not utopian, either. LeGuin's alternative society does not picture the good life and one may question whether it is even a better world. The Gethenian society is merely a means to raise questions about human nature and the human psyche, but LeGuin does not go so far as to provide definite answers.[15] This would, in her opinion, amount to escapism. In a comment on the science fiction short story anthology *Again, Dangerous Visions*, edited by Harlan Ellison in 1972, LeGuin appreciates that American science fiction authors have started to deal with relevant problems such as racism, sexism, militarism, prejudice, pollution and so forth, but she deplores the "savagely self-

---

[14]Suvin, "On the Poetics of the Science Fiction Genre," p. 375.
[15]Cf. LeGuin, "Is Gender Necessary?" p. 168.

righteous tone, a tone that implies that there's an answer, a simple answer."[16] She goes on to state:

> Well, I call this escapism: a sensationalist raising of a real question, followed by a quick evasion of the weight and pain and complexity involved in really, experientially, trying to understand and cope with that question . . . . If science fiction has a major gift to offer literature, I think it is just this: the capacity to face an open universe. Physically open, psychically open.[17]

This call for openness can be found on the structural as well as on the thematic levels in *The Left Hand of Darkness*. Obviously, LeGuin seems to believe that an author has a moral obligation in creating her/his literature. She herself intends to treat aspects of human life which she considers important and to stimulate reflection about them. Her need to rethink the meanings of gender and sexuality did not result in a lecture but in an effort to hint at the multitudinous aspects and implications of sex-role behavior. Thus, her Gethenians are "questions, not answers; process, not stasis."[18] She goes on to state in her essay "Is Gender Necessary?":

> One of the essential functions of science fiction, I think, is precisely this kind of question-asking: reversals of an habitual way of thinking, metaphors for what our language has no words for as yet, experiments in imagination.[19]

LeGuin claims that the major subject of the book is betrayal and fidelity, and not gender, sexuality, and feminism.[20] In *The Left Hand of Darkness*, however, betrayal and fidelity as ways of human interaction are inextricably linked to the implications and consequences of the sex/gender problem. Some critics have justly claimed that the actual plot of *The Left Hand of Darkness* is neither based on the hermaphroditic nature of the Gethenians, nor does it reflect this fact.[21] In my opinion it is possible to connect Genly Ai's character development to his recognition of the meaning of androgyny and gender. One can further argue that his initial mistrust of Estraven stems from his rejection of the feminine qualities in him, and only when he can accept these and see Estraven whole, can his mission

---

[16]Ursula K. LeGuin, "On Teaching Science Fiction," in *Teaching Science Fiction: Education for Tomorrow*, J. Williamson, ed. (Philadelphia: Owlswick Press, 1980), p. 24.
[17]*ibid.*, pp. 24-25.
[18]LeGuin, "Is Gender Necessary?" p. 163.
[19]*ibid.*
[20]*ibid.*, p. 162. In her latest essay collection *Dancing at the Edge of the World: Thoughts on Words, Women, Places* (New York: Grove Press, 1989), LeGuin includes a reprint of "Is Gender Necessary?" with a running commentary in bracketed italics, which is to reflect her changes of mind during the last decade. She asks everyone who wants to quote from this essay to include these reconsiderations. A I wrote this study before I had access to LeGuin's new edition of her much-quoted text, I shall respect her request in rendering her new commentaries in the appropriate footnotes, to which I would draw the reader's attention. In this instance, she states in her commentary that she "was feeling defensive, and resentful that critics of the book insisted upon talking only about its 'gender problems,' as if it were an essay not a novel." She is aware that "there are other aspects to the book, which are involved with its sex-gender aspects quite inextricably." (LeGuin, *Dancing at the Edge of the World*, p. 8.)
[21]See e.g. David Ketterer, "Ursula K. LeGuin's Archetypal 'Winter-Journey,'" in *Ursula K. LeGuin*, H. Bloom, ed., p. 14.

succeed. Nevertheless, there remains a discrepancy between imaginative world and plot which may relegate Gethenian hermaphroditism to the exotic background atmosphere of the novel. For the purpose of this study, however, I shall neglect the main story line and concentrate on the conception of Gethenian society for which it is valid that LeGuin's thrust is directed at sex-role behavior:

> Because of our lifelong social conditioning, it is hard for us to see clearly what, besides purely physiological form and function, truly differentiates men and women. Are there real differences in temperament, capacity, talent, psychic processes, etc.? . . . I eliminated gender, to find out what was left.[22]

This reductive method in her thought-experiment leads her to the use of one of the oldest and most wide-spread myths and archetypes of humanity, namely androgyny. The concept of androgyny contains the combination of masculinity and femininity in one person. Originally this included the biological level as well. In our contemporary culture, however, androgyny is regarded as a predominantly psychological phenomenon. I shall use it in this sense here whereas the term "hermaphroditism" will be used to refer to biological and physiological ambisexuality. In accord with this differentiation between the biological/physical and psychological levels I shall use "sex" for reference to the biological phenomenon of maleness and femaleness. "Gender" will be reserved for the social constructs of masculinity and femininity, which do not always appear symmetrically with their biological counterparts. According to this terminology, LeGuin eliminated not only gender in her Gethenians, but sex as well. She thus transcended sex/gender dualism in her imagination in order to look at what she perceives to be people's androgynous psychology.

* * *

The myth of the androgyne is a world-wide phenomenon and can directly be linked to the mythical Golden Age and the yearning for a lost harmony. The anthropologist Hermann Baumann traces the parallelism of the heaven-earth and male-female dichotomy back to creation myths which are related to androgyny:

> The appearance of Heaven and Earth as a united couple, either divided into two individual partners from the beginning, or having sprung from a later division of an originally bisexual entity ("Myth of the division of Heaven and Earth," "Egg of the World") constitute the leitmotif of the "Myth of the World". The opposition Heaven-Earth is only one pair of terms . . . , in a series of other such pairs which divides the world into opposites . . . . If the bisexual original universe [Urkosmos] is halved, an "Above" and a "Below" will come into existence; if the bisexual original human being is divided, it will be split into a right male and a left female side. The right-left polarity thus runs parallel to male-female, above-below, warm-cold, light-dark, dry-wet and all the other opposites.[23]

---

[22]LeGuin, "Is Gender Necessary?" p. 163.

[23]Hermann Baumann, *Das Doppelte Geschlecht: Studien zur Bisexualität in Ritus und Mythos* (Berlin: Reimer, 1986) p. 252. Author's translation.

All of the polarities listed here recur as motifs throughout *The Left Hand of Darkness*.[24] It is very likely that LeGuin knew and used these anthropological data because the title of her novel already topicalizes the right-left polarity which is central to the idea of androgyny. *The Left Hand of Darkness* is taken from the beginning of "Tormer's Lay", a piece of Karhidish folklore:

> Light is the left hand of darkness,
> and darkness the right hand of light.
> Two are one, life and death, lying
> together like lovers in kemmer,
> like hands joined together, like
> the end and the way.
> (*The Left Hand of Darkness*, p. 164)

Many cultures apply the right/male/heaven and left/female/earth polarity to the human body. This has led to the belief that the right side is the important side of men and the left the appropriate one for women, and often certain activities may only be done with the right or the left hand respectively. The belief behind such ideas is that men and women are always androgynous due to their right and left halves. One side prevails to determine a person's sex and so becomes his or her "right" side.[25] As most cultures and societies are patriarchal, the right side and its concomitant aspects are more highly valued than their left counterparts. Matriarchal societies tend to place a higher value on the left/earth/female pole.[26] LeGuin has reversed right and left in "Tormer's Lay", associating right with darkness and the female/earth polarity, while the left is related to light and the male pole. This, however, cannot simply be interpreted as a means of elevating the female pole, attempting to indicate the raised status of female-related associations. As Baumann points out, those cultures which deviate from the general pattern which he has outlined are the Chinese culture, where in the Yin-Yang school the right side is associated with the female pole and the left side with the male one, and the culture of certain Prairie-Indian tribes which are particularly belligerent and which equate the right male side with war and death and the left female side with life and peace, thus emphasizing the latter as the better one despite their patriarchal organization.[27] Those are also the cultures in which LeGuin and her father A.L. Kroeber show most interest. This elaborate use of anthropological data in the construction of her alternative society points to the considerable possibilities of the science fiction genre.

* * *

In order to return to the origin of the novel as stated at the beginning of this section, namely that it was written in the wake of the New Feminism, it is worth considering that the androgyne has been an ideal for some parts of the Women's Movement. Carolyn G. Heilbrun's *Toward a Recognition of Androgyny* (1973) and June Singer's *Androgyny: Towards a New Theory of Sexuality* (1976) are proof of

---

[24]See, for instance, David Lake, "LeGuin's Twofold Vision: Contrary Image-Sets in *The Left Hand of Darkness*," *Science Fiction Studies*, 8 (1981) pp. 156-163.
[25]Baumann, *Das doppelte Geschlecht*, pp. 293-310. See in particular p. 303: "In his/her opposite limbs every human being possesses something of the opposite sex." (Author's translation)
[26]*ibid.*, p. 296.
[27]*ibid.*, pp. 295-296 *et passim*.

the popularity of androgyny at the time. It symbolized the transcending of gender and the possibility of a utopian society:

> I believe that our future salvation lies in a movement away from sexual polariza-
> tion and the prison of gender toward a world in which individual roles and modes of
> personal behavior can be freely chosen. The ideal toward which I believe we should
> move is best described by the term "androgyny". This ancient Greek word - from
> *andro* (male) and *gyn* (female) - defines a condition under which the characteristics of
> the sexes and the human impulses expressed by men and women, are not rigidly as-
> signed. Androgyny seeks to liberate the individual from the confines of the appro-
> priate.[28]

Carolyn Heilbrun implied in this definition that androgyny might lead to a re-
conciliation of the sexes and open up the full range of human reactions and experiences for both of them.[29]
This kind of androgyny on the psychic level is what LeGuin had in mind when
she wrote *The Left Hand of Darkness*. She says about the "archetype of the Androgyne":

> I do feel that it is one of the archetypes/potentialities of the human psyche which
> is of real importance now and full of creative-destructive energy, ..., The Androgyne
> theme in my book is surely related to such phenomena as the women's movement and
> gay lib, and unisex clothes, and many other portents.[30]

Obviously, in LeGuin's opinion androgyny is related to equality. In the same
way as Charlotte Perkins Gilman argued in her novel *Herland* that the equality of
the sexes is potentially given in the present, LeGuin seems to consider human
beings equal psychologically already, here and now. There is a difference in sex
but not in gender. This is what she wants to emphasize in *The Left Hand of Darkness*:

> Yes, indeed the people in it are androgynous, but that doesn't mean that I'm pre-
> dicting that in a millenium or so we will all be androgynous, or announcing that I
> think we damned well ought to be androgynous. I'm merely observing, in the peculiar,
> devious, and thought-experimental manner proper to science fiction, that if you look
> at us at certain odd times of day in certain wheathers, we already are. I am not pre-
> dicting, or prescribing . . . . I am describing certain aspects of psychological reality in
> the novelist's way, which is by inventing elaborately circumstantial lies. (*The Left
> Hand of Darkness*, ix-x)

If we recognize that the sexes are basically equal already, equality for women
will be the only logical consequence. LeGuin, however, is not as ardently concerned with politics as is Gilman. Whereas Gilman attempted to show that women are able to create an orderly and effective utopian society, LeGuin explored

---

[28]Carolyn G. Heilbrun, Introduction to *Toward a Recognition of Androgyny* (New York: Alfred A.
Knopf, 1973) pp. ix-x.
[29]*ibid.*, pp. x-xi.
[30]Ursula K. LeGuin, "Ketterer on *The Left Hand of Darkness*," *Science Fiction Studies*, 2,2 (1975) p.
138. As LeGuin has stated that she had not read C.G. Jung when she wrote *The Left Hand of
Darkness*, I shall neglect the Jungian discussion of androgyny (see "Is Gender Necessary?" pp. 167-
168).

how the world would look to an androgynous mind and how this view would differ from a mind determined by gender indentity.

This attempt to describe an androgynous outlook on the world links androgyny to another important theme in the novel: unity. This unity, however, is not one which excludes other aspects or opposites. It is a concept of unity which aims at the harmonious integration of diverse aspects and at the creation of balance. In a conversation during the Gobrin Ice Trek the protagonists explore the difference of outlook in their minds - Genly, the man, and Estraven, the hermaphrodite, the physical symbol of androgyny:

> Ai brooded, and after some time he said, "You're isolated, and undivided. Perhaps you are as obsessed with wholeness as we are with dualism."
> "We are dualists, too. Duality is an essential, isn't it? So long as there is *myself* and *the other*."
> "I and Thou," he said. "Yes, it does, after all, go even wider than sex . . ."
> (*The Left Hand of Darkness*, p. 164)

The idea of unity as a theme in *The Left Hand of Darkness* is most strongly expressed in the Handdara religion of Karhide, of which Estraven is an adept. Almost all critics have commented on the fact that the Handdara religion is modelled on Taoism and the Yin-Yang-school of thought by which LeGuin is influenced.[31] This will be more explicitly discussed in part 3. I shall only mention here that androgyny can be related to Taoism and that the Yin-Yang-symbol also reflects the idea of androgyny in its representation of the perfect balance of the female/dark/earth and male/light/heaven poles.[32]

* * *

On the structural level LeGuin's concept of unity is reflected in the complex interrelation of the book's various chapters. *The Left Hand of Darkness* consists of twenty chapters told by various narrators. Genly Ai is the "ordering consciousness" behind the story. He says in the opening chapter:

> The story is not all mine, nor told by me alone. Indeed I am not sure whose story it is; you can judge better. But it is all one, and if at moments facts seem to alter with an altered voice, why then you can choose the fact you like best; yet none of them are false, and it is all one story. (*The Left Hand of Darkness*, p. 1)

This programmatic declaration appears at the beginning of the novel as introduction to the story and is presented as part of a documentary report. The other voices in the novel are: Estraven, the investigator Tot Ong Oppong of the first Ekumenical landing party on Gethen, tellers of folklore tales, a creation myth, and a sermon of the Yomesh religious canon.

The fourteen chapters which are narrated by Genly Ai and Estraven carry the action and the novel's plot. Sometimes the reader is informed about the same set

---

[31]As examples for criticism which deals especially with this topic, see Barbour, "Wholeness and Balance;" Dena C. Bain, "The 'Tao te Ching' as Background to the Novels of Ursula K. LeGuin," in *Ursula K. LeGuin*, H. Bloom, ed., pp. 211-224. LeGuin called herself "an unconsistent Taoist and a consistent unChristian" in "Ketterer on *The Left Hand of Darkness*," p. 139.

[32]See Peter Thiele, "Yin und Yang," in *Androgyn: Sehnsucht nach Vollkommenheit*, Neuer Berliner Kunstverein, ed. (Berlin: Reimer, 1986) pp. 251-254.

of events from their different perspectives, so that the story takes the form of parallel accounts which sometimes partly overlap.

The five chapters of Gethenian folklore are interspersed throughout the main story and contribute considerably to the necessary background information of LeGuin's alternative world. Their placing seems to be arbitrary and seemingly disruptive to the plot. They do, however, help the reader to decode the different codes of communication and personal relationships on Gethen. In the first chapter, for instance, the reader puzzles with Genly about the curious behavior of Estraven and his opponent, the king's cousin, who succeeds in denouncing Estraven as a traitor and in forcing him into exile. This chapter is followed by a Hearth tale about two brothers and their forbidden incestuous relationship. Although the content of this story bears no reflection to the first chapter, it does become obvious that the Gethenians have a completely different code of honor and a different set of values to regulate their relationships. Only very much later in the novel, when Estraven's incestuous kemmer relationship to his brother is mentioned, will this chapter become necessary in order to interprete and understand this relationship and its meaning with regard to the characterization of Estraven. LeGuin uses this method of back-reference generally in *The Left Hand of Darkness*, so that the tales help the reader to understand what has been going on immediately before, although they unfold their full explanatory content later in the novel.

The seventh chapter, told by the Investigator who explains Gethenian physiology and its social implications, does not so much help to clarify the story itself. It is necessary, however, for the understanding of the empirical and scientific side of LeGuin's imaginary world. In providing this information in this way, LeGuin circumvents the kind of didactic dialogue which one almost always finds in utopias, when the visitor is initiated into a different society by his mentor.

This web of fragments which constitutes plot and alternative world alike exemplifies a unity which has grown out of diversity. Various myths mirror the action and explain the alternative world. Different narrators, using different dictions (journal, report, saga), provide several points of view and see the same event from different angles. LeGuin does not allow any one perspective to become absolute, since she sees truth as relative. The subjective aspect of a point of view is accepted and either/or-logic is denied.[33] Genly Ai, who develops and changes as a character during the novel, is the "omniscient ordering principle",[34] but his account of the action is complemented by that of Estraven. This reflects the bacis theme of duality in unity, related to androgyny and the Yin-Yang-school. Moreover, Genly includes the Investigator's notes as well as Gethenian myths and tales. The latter contrast his voice and Estraven's and so build another dual unity into the story. So Genly allows the multiple point of view in an act of power sharing.[35] The different narrative perspectives also keep the reader from accepting any single point of view too easily. This leads to a certain estrangement which prevents simple answers to the questions raised by LeGuin in *The Left Hand of Darkness*, and at the same time stimulates reflection about our own way

[33]Cf. Heinz Tschachler, "Ursula LeGuin: *The Left Hand of Darkness*," in *Der Science-Fiction Roman in der angloamerikanischen Literatur, Interpretationen*, H. Heuermann, ed. (Düsseldorf: Bagel, 1986) pp. 295-314.
[34]Peter Brigg, "The Archetype of the Journey in Ursula K. LeGuin's Fiction," in *Ursula K. LeGuin*, Olander and Greenberg, eds., p. 50.
[35]Tschachler, "Ursula LeGuin," p. 306.

of life.[36] The many parallels in the story line as well as the parallels of myth and reality challenge the reader to put the pieces together. Linearity in the narrated time is juxtaposed to mythical time and also there is a circularity in the novel as it begins in the Karhidish capital, Erhenrang, with a key-stone ceremony which prefigures the joining of Gethen and the Ekumen in the end.[37] By leaving the ending open, LeGuin does not propose a utopian ending for Gethen.

* * *

In *The Left Hand of Darkness*, the themes of unity and androgyny permeate each other and even bear upon the structural level. LeGuin's imaginative model of society is rather unique in science fiction writing. The only precedent is Theodore Sturgeon's *Venus Plus X* (1960).[38] In this novel there exists an undiscovered world adjacent to this one called Ledom (reverse of "model"). Its inhabitants transform themselves surgically into hermaphrodites because they regard gender dichotomy as socially detrimental. They are confronted by a contemporary American male who, upon discovering this custom, reacts with hostility and disgust. Sturgeon thus aimed in the same direction as LeGuin. He remained, however, much more didactic and did not make Ledom as extensively coherent as LeGuin's Gethen. The possibility of surgical hermaphroditism makes his utopian Ledom more practical than LeGuin's alien Gethen, which is really just a mental game. As a piece of feminist writing, *The Left Hand of Darkness* is regarded by feminist critics as a tentative beginning with several flaws in its imagined world due to the lack of feminist theoretical tenets. It is nevertheless important since it is, after all, one the the first science fiction novels written by women with feminist concerns and the imagination of a world without gender differentiation.[39]

2.2 Marge Piercy: *Woman on the Edge of Time*

Marge Piercy's novel *Woman on the Edge of Time* appeared in 1976, eight years after the publication of *The Left Hand of Darkness*. The Women's Movement had made considerable impact on U.S. society by then. Unlike LeGuin, Marge Piercy has been a political activist in the New Left since the late fifties. In her essay "The Grand Coolie Damn"(1969) she described how she realized that sexism and male chauvinism were dominating characteristics of the male leadership of the New Left, and how she therefore joined the Women's Movement.[40]

As a writer, Piercy is deeply and consciously influenced by her politics. In her mind, writing is a form of political activism because art is a part of the living society and not an abstract ideal for intellectuals:

---

[36]Keinhorst, *Utopien von Frauen*, p. 57.

[37]Tschachler, "Ursula LeGuin," p. 295.

[38]For the following discussion of *Venus Plus X* see Annas, "New Worlds, New Words," pp. 147-148; Beverly Friend, "Virgin Territory: Women and Sex in Science Fiction," *Extrapolation*, 14 (1972) pp. 53-54.

[39]June Howard, "Widening the Dialogue on Feminist Science Fiction," in *Feminist Revisions: What Has Been And What Might Be*, Patraka and Tilly, eds. (Ann Arbor: The University of Michigan, Women's Studies Program, 1983) p. 67.

[40]Marge Piercy, "The Grand Coolie Damn," in *Sisterhood is Powerful: An Anthology of Writings from the Women's Liberation Movement*, R. Morgan, ed. (New York: Vintage, 1970) pp. 473-492.

> The notion that politics have nothing to do with art is a very modern heresy . . . .
> For most of the world's history, poets have thought of themselves as human beings in
> a social web, with the same duties in the public sphere as anyone else, with the same
> set of human interests. My art is political, but no more political than a lot of art not so
> labeled, which also contains strong notions about what's immoral, moral, what's good
> and bad, having and getting, who's smart and who's stupid.[41]

Obviously, Piercy's notion of the politics of art differs from LeGuin's, who does not view the writer as a political activist and who percieves her realm to be philosophical. Both women, however, believe that writers have a moral obligation towards their audience, they have to use their own imagination in order to stimulate a thought process in the reader.

Piercy always aims at political awareness. Her first two novels deal with experiences in the early New Left, whereas her third novel, *Small Changes* (1973), centers on the early new Women's Movement and the beginning consciousness raising of women.

Woman on the Edge of Time is Piercy's fourth novel and her only venture into the area of utopian or science fiction writing. She says about her book:

> *Woman on the Edge of Time* is my favorite of my novels. I simply think it's the best
> I've done so far. My first intent was to create an image of a good society, one that was
> *not* sexist, racist, or imperialist: one that *was* cooperative, respectful of all living
> beings, gentle, responsible, loving and playful. The result of a full feminist revolution.
> To try to imagine people of such a society was my hardest task.[42]

In *Woman on the Edge of Time* the protagonist Consuelo Ramos, called Connie, a poor, middle-aged Chicana living in a New York slum, is delivered to a psychiatric clinic by the pimp of her niece Dolly, because she attacked him in an attempt to defend and protect Dolly. At the same time, she is contacted by a person from a future time. We learn that this person, Luciente from the utopian society of Mattapoisett of the year 2137, has visited the bewildered Connie a few times before the action of the novel begins.

While Connie is unjustly transferred to a state mental hospital, drugged, treated badly, and never taken seriously, Luciente periodically takes her into her future world which is an egalitarian and idyllic "ecotopia".[43] Every time she goes there, Connie learns more about this strange society, and gradually her initial skepticism and rejection give way to understanding and acceptance. Meanwhile, she is chosen for a project in which brain surgery (amygdalotomy and the implantation of electrodes into the brain) is to be tested as a means of controlling the patients' behavior and emotions. Connie tries to escape but she is soon captured again. When the operations on her brain begin, she once tries to reach Luciente but ends up in a dystopian alternative future instead, and in her visits to Luciente's future Connie participates in a war in which the enemies of Luciente's Mattapoisett turn out to be the physicians who perform the experiments on her. She begins to understand that she has to struggle in order to make Luciente's fu-

[41]Celia Betsky, "Talk with Marge Piercy," *The New York Times Book Review* (24th February 1980) p. 37.
[42]Marge Piercy, "Mirror Images," in *Women's Culture: The Women's Renaissance of the Seventies*, G. Kimball, ed. (Metuchen: Scarecrow, 1981) p. 193.
[43]Title of a utopian novel by Ernest Callenbach, *Ecotopia: A Novel About Ecology, People and Politics in 1999* (1975), in which ecological consciousness is very important.

ture happen and to prevent the other dystopian future from coming into existence. When she is allowed to visit her brother for Christmas and realizes that he will not help her to get out of the mental hospital, she steals poison from him and kills her physicians.

* * *

Piercy's book actually contains two novels because equal care and space is given to the story of Connie's life in the mental hospital as well as to the description of utopian Mattapoisett. Reviewers have suggested that the story is overburdened and Piercy overambitious.[44] In my opinion this criticism is valid. For the purpose of this study, however, I shall concentrate on the design for the alternative utopian future society.

Even though *Woman on the Edge of Time* is divided between two stories, it can be classified as a modern utopia as considerable weight is placed on the description of Mattapoisett, which is constructed according to the conditions proposed in part 1.1. Piercy's utopia is almost anachronistic because, as we have seen, contemporary utopian writing has become almost completely absorbed in the science fiction genre. Marge Piercy's Mattapoisett, however, stands firmly in the tradition of modern utopian writing as outlined in part 1.1. Thus, *Woman on the Edge of Time* is conventional rather than innovative. Unlike LeGuin, who effectively evaded the didacticism inherent in the utopian genre by using multiple voices and myths (although, as we have seen, her aim was not to create a utopia) Piercy relied heavily on the traditional visitor-guide pattern which dates as far back as More's *Utopia* and the early travel tales. Each time Connie is taken into the future by her guide and mentor Luciente, she is taught a new lesson about the structure and functioning of this future society: about living arrangements, interpersonal relationships, economy and ecology, government, education and childraising, the coordination of work, but also about art, festivals and rituals.

Feminist critics such as Keinhorst maintain that Piercy managed to keep the dialogue between Connie and Luciente, which mainly carries the depiction, lively and free from dullness, whereas others found these conversations longwinded and overly didactic.[45] In reviewing *Woman on the Edge of Time*, Margaret Atwood, for instance, admits the dullness of the dialogues but contends that they are indigenous to the utopian genre. The shortcomings are therefore in the form and not in the author.[46] However, she judges quite correctly: "Piercy expends a good deal of energy trying to get every last detail *in*, to get it *right*, and to make rather too sure we get the point."[47] Piercy's emphasis in her effort to portray a utopian society in such detail is in on the people, on how they live and feel, and how they relate to each other and their surroundings. In this she differs from her male precursors such as Bellamy, for example, who mainly described the *functioning* of his future society: what does the governmental hierarchy look like? how are people allocated to their work? how is the distribution of goods handled technically? The ensuing dialogues between the visitor Julian West and his guide Dr. Leete are therefore much more "objective", abstract, impersonal, and theo-

---

[44]Celia Betsky, Review of*Woman on the Edge of Time*, *The New Republic* (9th October 1976) p. 39.
[45]See Keinhorst, *Utopien von Frauen*, p. 111.
[46]Margaret Atwood, "Marge Piercy: *Woman on the Edge of Time, Living in the Open*," in *Second Words: Selected Critical Prose* (Boston: Beacon Press, 1982) p. 273. This review was originally published in *The Nation* (4th December 1976) pp. 601-602.
[47]*ibid.*, p. 275.

retical, than those between Connie and Luciente. Piercy always tries to move personal relationships into the foreground. As an example, Connie learns about the way children are raised in Mattapoisett by getting to know Luciente's daughter Dawn. Connie is reminded of her own daughter Angelina, who was taken away from her after she had abused her physically in a state of stress caused by her social problems. Thus, both women are emotionally involved in the discussion, which reflects their personal experiences and attitudes and never ends up on the impersonal level of a tract about ideal education. Since the self-confident Luciente is convinced of the superiority of her society and Connie is relegated to the role of pupil-to-be-convinced, Piercy is not able to avoid a certain sermonizing, to which the utopian genre is indeed prone.

Also, this method of concentrating on the immediate surroundings and on the people which Connie is able to meet, does not allow Piercy to present her conception of the future on a grand scale. Neither does the reader learn about a geographically wider organization and coordination of society, nor does Piercy elaborate on how her utopian future came into existence. As we have seen in the discussion of the modern utopia, the "historical" outline is important because it both constitutes part of the justification of the utopia in question and illuminates some of the pragmatic ways of establishing it. It is therefore regrettable that Piercy did not give enough space to the history of Mattapoisett because she, like Bellamy, considers her utopia practicable:

> Certainly, I consider *Woman on the Edge of Time* speculative fiction. I set out to write a non-utopian utopia - that is, the utopia that is quite accessible with very close to present levels of technology. Although with nothing like present levels of political development. It is a place you could get to from here. It would take work, but it is quite doable.[48]

Obviously, *Woman on the Edge of Time* is supposed to stimulate the readers' political awareness, to interest them in our present political, social, and ecological problems, and to point to the fact that these can be remedied. *Woman on the Edge of Time* is therefore a social utopia which is related to Herbert Marcuse's criticism of society and his claim that the present society already possesses *all* means of creating utopia.[49]

Technology and science are part of these means, therefore Mattapoisett is not "technophobic". Dull and heavy work, such as dish-washing or the production of machinery, is fully automatized. So is human reproduction - a very important fact which will be fully discussed in part 3. Technology is used in education, and genetic engineering is applied to food-production (Luciente is a plant geneticist). In general, however, Piercy does not discuss science and technology at great length.[50]

Mattapoisett is a more past than future oriented utopia. Like Morris's artisans in *News from Nowhere*, the people of Mattapoisett indulge in the creativity of cooking, handicrafts, and needlework, and they all participate in agricultural work as part of their relationship to nature.

---

[48]Marge Piercy, Interview with Janice Bogstad, *Aurora*, 7,1 (1981) p. 5. Quoted after Keinhorst, *Utopien von Frauen*, pp. 91, 203.

[49]Cf. Göttner-Abendroth, "Der unversöhnliche Traum," pp. 7-8.

[50]Therefore, and because science is not topicalized in the way Suvin outlined as a condition of science fiction, the occasional classification of *Woman on the Edge of Time* as sience fiction is not appropriate.

In the characterization of her future people Piercy fulfills another criterion of the modern utopia. They are not uniform but highly individualistic, each with an individual life-style, special interests and personal traits. They are not, however, created as rounded characters but are intended merely to represent the whole spectrum of possible human personalities which can supposedly develop fully in utopian surroundings.

* * *

Since the character traits and interests of the people of Mattapoisett are not connected to sex/gender, they are androgynes in the sense of Heilbrun's definition. No activity is reserved for one of the sexes, no particular character traits and inclinations are expected from a person just because of her/his sex. This extends even to motherhood: because human reproduction is extracorporeal and automatized, men can be mothers. The concept of motherhood is valued highly in this society and it is connected to human characteristics which can best be acquired along with the experience of motherhood. Gilman's women in *Herland* hold a similar view when they claim that they are all mothers and that this is the source of their caring and nurturing attitude. In Piercy's utopia, motherhood is shared by women with men explicitly in order to humanize them. So Luciente tells Connie:

> It was part of women's long revolution. When we were breaking all the old hierarchies. Finally there was that one thing we had to give up too, the only power we ever had, in return for no more power for anyone. The original production: to give birth. Cause as long as we were biologically enchained, we'd never be equal. *And males never would be humanized to be loving and tender. So we all became mothers. Every child has three. To break the nuclear bonding.*[51]

It is interesting to note that for Piercy's utopian androgynes biological manipulation is necessary, although the transformation is not nearly as extensive as LeGuin's creation of hermaphroditic aliens. Women no longer bear children, men get hormonal treatment which will enable them to suckle the babies. Thus, the concept of androgyny is not regarded as a matter of the psychic level alone, for which LeGuin used the symbol of hermaphroditism, but psyche and physiology are perceived as interacting here.

Androgyny is not a central theme in *Woman on the Edge of Time*, as it is in *The Left Hand of Darkness*, and the word is never mentioned throughout the novel. Piercy, however, does play with its implications. When Connie is first visited by Luciente, she assumes that Luciente is a man because of her unselfconscious authority, her calloused hands which indicate that she works, and her way of moving about freely. Luciente's physical appearance and dress do not indicate her sex, i.e. she is not "made up". Connie, upon discovering that Luciente is a woman, reacts with surprise and anger similar to Genly Ai's confusion at the recognition of the feminine side of Estraven's nature. Prior to this discovery, she considered Luciente to be a "queer" because of her "girlish" manner and effeminate voice. Afterwards she compares her to "dykes" because of her muscular physique and her self-security. Obviously, this confusion arises when a gender-determined mind is confronted with androgyny, where gender-stereotypes cannot be applied. Most of the people Connie meets in Mattapoisett, however, can be clearly distinguished

---

[51]Marge Piercy, *Woman on the Edge of Time* (New York: Fawcett Crest, 1976) p. 105. Emphasis added. Subsequent references to this edition will be placed in parentheses in the text.

sexually. Androgyny is a social and psychological matter, not one of appearance (apart from the necessary physiological "corrections" mentioned above).

* * *

Linked to this egalitarian androgyny is the theme of matriarchal values which is implied on the one hand in the high value of "mothering" and on the other in the orientation towards the past in Piercy's utopia - matriarchy is often regarded as a mythical Golden Age by feminists.[52] In Mattapoisett women have given up the power of original reproduction on which the power and dominance of matriarchal women presumably rested, but the society is based on a value-system very different from our own, namely a "matriarchal" one. Women do not simply act like men do or are given access to male privileges, but both sexes are affected by the new value-system. Heide Göttner-Abendroth, who has engaged extensively in research about lost matriarchal cultures, says about their evocation:

> Impressive images of a wholly different femininity are evoked: Women full of erotic power and full of the knowledge of natural and psychic connections, powerful and exerting influence on the people around them.[53]

This witch-image applies to the women in Luciente's world - not so much to Luciente herself, but to Diana, Erzulia, or to the crone witches Sappho and White Oak. It is not restricted to women alone but the presentation of women as powerful characters is more striking that the association of natural and magical forces with men.

Göttner-Abendroth in this context mentions agricultural communes founded by women who emphasize an autarchic economy and who view agriculture, handicrafts, and arts as necessities of a life in harmony with nature. The life-style is simple and concentrates on inner peace and tenderness in human interaction. Unlike the people of Mattapoisett, these women reject technology completely.[54] It is worth mentioning in this context that the well-known U.S. community "Twin Oaks" features many of these traits but includes technology. It is not, however, a feminist community and includes men, thus coming rather close to Mattapoisett in various aspects which will be dealt with in part 3.[55]

Göttner-Abendroth admits that the present knowledge about matriarchal cultures is not sufficient to outline their basic structures and that any reconstructions are therefore necessarily mostly speculative.[56] Some feminists, however, do not regard the question of the actual existence of matriarchal societies as very important but point to the fact that the idea of matriarchy, i.e. the possibility of a culture in which women are powerful, is important in itself.[57] Göttner-Abendroth emphasizes the new definition of femininity

---

[52] Cf. Göttner-Abendroth, "Der unversöhnliche Traum," p. 5.

[53] *ibid.*, p. 14. Author's translation.

[54] *ibid.*, p. 15.

[55] See Weinbaum, "Twin Oaks," pp. 157-167.

[56] Göttner-Abendroth, "Der unversöhnliche Traum," pp. 14-15.

[57] As one example, see Margot Adler, "Meanings of Matriarchy," in *The Politics of Women's Spirituality*, Ch. Spretnak, ed. (Garden City, N.Y.: Anchor/Doubleday, 1982) pp. 127-137.

which plays a role here. Or the integration of masculinity in this new term of femininity . . . . Because here the issue could also be the rediscovery of man before his patriarchal self-mutilation.[58]

Piercy is greatly concerned with the values Göttner-Abendroth connects with matriarchy, but she does not topicalize matriarchy in an obvious way (nor does she topicalize androgyny). Instead, she is very careful to avoid any dominance of one sex over the other. Sex-role reversal is not the content of matriarchy but only a fear of men. Keinhorst found out that there are relatively few utopias with matriarchal features (i.e. a society of men *and* women, as opposed to unisex Amazonian conceptions) written by women, whereas matriarchy in the form of the sex-role reversal model has been used by many male writers, who usually depict the women as extremely malicious and sadistic towards the suppressed men. Sam Moskowitz collected several of these in his anthology *When Women Rule* (1972).[59] Such negative projections can be explained as fear or guilt on the men's side. Generally, women in feminist utopias are never interested in power over men or in their oppression.[60]

* * *

Let me conclude this general introduction to *Woman on the Edge of Time* by returning to my initial remark that it is in a way "anachronistic": As we have seen in part 1.3, women writers did not appropriate the utopian genre in the same way as their male colleagues did. This was partly due to their limited prospects and restricted hopes as women. It is interesting in this context to note that science fiction women writers are almost always found at the utopian pole of science fiction, using the potential of this genre in order to create alternative societies in which women are valued. Pamela Annas asks:

> Why did women writers choose not to work in this genre until very recently? One good reason is the potentially revolutionary form. In order to build paradigms of an alternative vision of reality, a writer needs to have a fairly secure base from which to build and some sense of what is possible. She needs either a *tradition* into which she fits as a writer or, more generally, as a member of a class, or she needs a *community* of some kind which shares enough of her basic assumptions. Either a tradition or a community is necessary in order to develop a dialectical awareness of oneself in relation to past and future.[61]

Although there exists a long list of women writers who have used the utopian tradition for a long time, as Daphne Patai has shown, this tradition has largely been ignored in literary history. Only recently has it surfaced again in feminist research.

Thus, when LeGuin entered this area in 1968 with *The Left Hand of Darkness*, she had neither a tradition nor a community to fall back on. (Neither did her precursors whom I discussed in part 1.3, with the exception of Gilman). This may account for the tentativeness of her alternative conception of society and its lack of

---

[58]Göttner-Abendroth, "Der unversöhnliche Traum," p. 14. Author's translation.

[59]Keinhorst, *Utopien von Frauen*, pp. 27-28.

[60]One exception is Marion Zimmer Bradley's *The Ruins of Isis* (1978). Men's bondage, however, is in the end rejected as degenerated.

[61]Annas, "New Worlds, New Words," p. 145.

a thorough feminist analysis. In 1974 she published her novel *The Dispossessed*, which portrays the future anarchic society of Anarres. LeGuin has remained in the analogic mode of science fiction by setting this society in the distant future on another planet. Its design is strongly utopian and in many ways close to Piercy's Mattapoisett. This may well be linked to the fact that by then a tradition of feminist utopias in science fiction had been established - Joanna Russ being the most important pioneer - and that feminist theory and the Women's Movement could provide the necessary community and the shared basic assumptions mentioned by Annas. Piercy herself has drawn considerably on Shulamith Firestone's *The Dialectic of Sex* (1970), a pioneer work of Radical Feminist theory.

Most of the women writers who attempt to create utopian alternative societies use the science fiction genre. Consequently these conceptions are not related to practicability but are to be regarded as thought-experiments and critiques of our society. Perhaps women are not yet able to envision a utopia for women (and men) which could actually be realized.

Woman on the Edge of Time is the only modern utopia in the sense used in this study ever written by a woman writer of the English language. For the first time a woman writer has been able to use this literary genre is a way in which men used it a long time ago, namely in order to project a better world. Therefore, in the light of feminist literature, *Woman on the Edge of Time* is a revolutionary novel. I do not intend here to argue that content in feminist literature is more important than style, as for instance Theresia Sauter-Bailliet did in her article "Marge Piercy: *Woman on the Edge of Time*" (1976). *Woman on the Edge of Time*, as we have seen, can well be criticized for several reasons. I do not think, however, that the simple fact that Piercy used an anachronistic genre which entails a conventional form, can be held against her as a major flaw, as for example Roger Sale did in his review in the *New York Times Book Review* (1976).[62] In the light of the fact that utopian writing by women has a different history from that by men, literary criticism ought to put *Woman on the Edge of Time* into this context rather than in the context of the contemporary literary scene alone. The standard against which *Woman on the Edge of Time* should best be compared and evaluated is provided by novels such as Bellamy's *Looking Backward*.

2.3 Sally Miller Gearhart: *The Wanderground. Stories of the Hill Women*

In 1979, when Sally Miller Gearhart's *The Wanderground* appeared, the Women's Movement was a very active factor on the American political scene. It had also evolved some theoretical positions. To this day, however, there is no one unified feminist theory, but several strands originating from various political, intellectual and/or philosophical backgrounds. Josephine Donovan, in her study *Feminist Theory: The Intellectual Traditions of American Feminism* (1985), categorizes and describes the different theoretical branches of feminist thought, their contexts and relationships to other political and/or philosophical movements as well as their interrelationships and their major authors and politicians.

Of the three writers who are mainly examined in this study, Gearhart can be most explicitly placed in a political context; she is obviously and acknowledgedly connected to the prevailing feminist theory in the U.S.A., namely Radical Feminism, and within this particular feminist theory Gearhart opts strongly for

---

[62]Roger Sale, Review of *Woman on the Edge of Time*, *The New York Times Book Review* (20th June 1976) p. 6.

one of its particular branches, Lesbian Separatism. As this includes a separation from men and patriarchal culture as far as possible (e.g. women's communes, women's collectives), it is not surprising that her utopian vision is an all-women one.

* * *

In Gearhart's novel *The Wanderground* the reader is confronted with a society of women who live in the wilderness without the help of technology. They have developed powerful spiritual and magical abilities instead. The subtitle of *The Wanderground, Stories of the Hill Women*, relates to the fact that there is no real plot and, although the stories are chronologically arranged, there is no linear narrative either. Almost every story is about a different woman, whom the reader accompanies through either a short journey, an encounter with somebody or something else, a mystic experience or just an everyday activity. There is, however, a thread running through the stories: The action, or actions, are set in the future; after "the Earth's revolt" (i.e. the Earth has created an energy which prevents exploitative technology from functioning) no "rape of the Earth", but no rape of woman either is possible outside the "cities", the centers of a patriarchal technocratic dystopia where women are degraded as mere sex-objects or birth-machines. During the course of the novel we learn that many have fled to the "hills" (or anywhere else, into the country) in order to escape an unbearable and increasing oppression of women in a dystopian future extrapolated from the gynophobic aspects of our present society. The women then developed their amazing metaphysical skills (e.g. telepathy, telekinesis, witchcraft, etc.) in a mystic unity with nature which even enables them to communicate with animals and plants - all of this renders technology superfluous.

They have also created a different social structure in which, similar to Piercy's design, there is no center of power. Decisions are made by all, no woman being forced to obey either another or a majority decision. There are no families and no one-on-one relationships (also regarded as "clipping" and "binding" in *Woman on the Edge of Time*). All of this transpires through the stories of the women meeting, communicating, feasting, travelling and so forth. Similarly, the reader is told about how and why the community of the hill women came into existence, how they keep in touch with the "city", and how they are threatened by its expanding "male energy". In the opening chapter a woman arrives at the Wanderground who, as we later learn, has been raped outside the city, where men are supposedly impotent. This threat is increased by the fact that men have undertaken raids in the area around the city in order to hunt animals just for the sake of killing.

The city is the dystopian antidote to the Wanderground. There is poverty, violence, crime, continual electronic surveillance of the citizens, a totalitarian, brutal regime which enforces stereotypical sex-role behavior. Women have no freedom and are not even allowed to go outside without male company - they may even have to take resort to a "rentscort". The hill women, in order to keep themselves informed about the state of the enemy city, send a certain number of women there on "rotation" for a particular time. These women disguise themselves as men.

The history of the origin of the Wanderground and the city are given in the memories of the old women who recall the beginnings. Furthermore, the women store and pass on such memories with the help of telepathy in the "remember-rooms". These memories, which tell of a twentieth-century-style witch hunt,

50

increasing violence against non-conformist women, and eventually of the "Revolt of the Earth", are part of every hill woman's education and determine her political attitude towards men.

Towards the end of the book the story culminates in a confrontation between the hill women and the "Gentles" (i.e. men who do not have sexual intercourse with women). Before they meet, The women have a quarrel concerning cooperation with the Gentles. The women regard men as the source of violence, as for example in their "invasion litany" which describes male attitude thus:

> *If it moves: shoot it down.*
> *If it grows: cut it.*
> *It is wild: tame it, claim it.*
> *If it flows: a harness.*
> *It shines or burns: gouge it out.*
> *It is female: rape it.*[63]

The women are aware of the fact that this simple dualism, male-evil vs. female-good, is simplistic: "It is too simple, . . . , to condemn them all or to praise all of us. But for the sake of earth and all she holds, that simplicity must be our creed."(*The Wanderground*, p. 2). This leads many of the women to reject men totally and to refuse to deal with any of them. So when the Gentles ask the women for a meeting, these women refuse to agree whereas others consider the Gentles to be loyal allies, particularly for the women on rotation. After a long argument the women agree that some of them may go to meet the Gentles on their own behalf, but not as representatives of all hill women.

At the meeting the Gentles inform the women that they found out that the violent male energy of the city is able to expand when the number of the hill women and other country women on rotation decreases. Furthermore they demonstrate their own newly developed mental skills which differ from the women's. The women's deep mistrust of them reflects, as did the quarrel among the women earlier, a question that has occupied and occasionally even split the Women's Movement: How should women deal with men? Should there be cooperation with men or not? Evona, one of the three women who have agreed to meet the Gentles, accuses them and, at the same time, all men:

> You've given me no reason to trust you . . . . How will you use that power [i.e. the Gentles' mental skills]? To pry into the lives of others? To conquer them? . . . . When have men ever used their power for anything else . . . . The whole raped world is a testimony to that." (*The Wanderground*, p. 179)

Although the meeting ends in a conciliatory mood, the mistrust remains.

In the last chapter one of the women, Artilidea, prepares for her dying in a ritual. It becomes clear that the women are pledged to non-violence - although their psychic powers would enable them to destroy the cities - and that they regard the saving of the earth as their main task:

> *To work as if the earth, the mother, can be saved.*
> *To work as if our healing care were not too late.*

---

[63]Sally Miller Gearhart, *The Wanderground. Stories of the Hill Women* (Watertown, Mass.: Persephone Press, 1979) p. 193. Subsequent references to this edition will be placed in parentheses within the text.

Work to stay the slayer's hand,
Helping him to change
Or helping him to die.
Work as if the earth, the mother, can be saved.
(The Wanderground, p. 195)

The Earth, however, does not answer the women's question as to whether it can be saved, leaving open the result of the women's struggle and the story itself.

* * *

The Wanderground is usually spoken of as a novel by critics, yet this is difficult to determine. The structure of the story-line is very loose. The book opens *in medias res* with a chapter/story simply called "Opening", which sets the tone of the novel as well as introducing some of its major themes. Little is explained, however, and the readers have to worm their way slowly into the curious language of the Wanderground (e.g. special terminology for metaphysical skills) and the many implications whose meaning will only be revealed much later in the novel. Even though the stories depend on one another for their full understanding, they are usually closed like short stories (in fact, some of them were published as such in journals prior to the publication of *The Wanderground*). Thus, on the formal level, *The Wanderground* is very loosely structured for a novel.

On the level of content, the structure is non-linear. Although the adventures of each heroine in every story are narrated in a chronological way and the stories are ordered according to a chronology of these mostly unrelated adventures, the history of the Wanderground is rendered in more or less arbitrary flashbacks. There is no obvious point of departure for the whole story, and there is no end: Although the novel ends with the image of a woman and a goat being escorted to the place of their dying - which would otherwise constitute a stereotypical ending - the underlying action is nowhere near its end. How the women are going to deal with the threat from the city, with the Gentles, or with the dying earth, is still open, and not every story contributes to these issues or to what I have formerly referred to as a "thread running through the stories." It is easily possible to imagine the novel expanded at either end by similar stories, as if there existed no linear narrative from A to B but as if we were presented with a random piece of an ongoing process. Sarah Lefanu has described *The Wanderground* as: "illustrative, discursive, non-developmental."[64]

* * *

This lack of a linear and directed structure reflects the underlying politics of anarchy and its rejection of any form of leadership and rigid organization. Even more important in this context is the use of a "cluster-protagonist"[65]:

There is no single heroine in *The Wanderground*; instead, the whole society of the hill women functions as protagonist. Lefanu observes: "The Wanderground is a portrait of a culture rather than of individuals."[66] The depiction of a culture

---

[64]Sarah Lefanu, *In the Chinks of the World Machine: Feminism and Science Fiction* (London: The Womens Press, 1988) p. 65.
[65]Keinhorst, *Utopien von Frauen*, p. 123.
[66]Lefanu, *In the Chinks of the World Machine*, p. 65.

rather than of multiple protagonists reflects an attitude of sharing which resembles LeGuin's choice to add various voices to Genly Ai's in *The Left Hand of Darkness*. In its refusal to center on one figure or group of figures, thus avoiding an ordering consciousness as is Genly Ai in *The Left Hand of Darkness*, it goes even further in the dissolution of a power hierarchy. The fact that the story is carried along by different heroines in each story relates to the concept of rotation of tasks which is central to anarchy and its major tenet, namely to avoid control of one person by another.[67] Authority and responsibility are to be distributed equally, rendering each person important and valuable. Thus, the impression is given that every woman partakes in the destiny of the society and contributes to it. There is no savior and no leader, as for example in *The Left Hand of Darkness* and, to a lesser extent, in *Woman on the Edge of Time*, which, however, in emphasizing Connie's development, clings to the concept of the developing protagonist. Gearhart herself emphasizes strongly and repeatedly the importance of non-hierarchical relationships, of which she considers women to be naturally more capable as men, in her essays. She also considers women to be naturally more strongly oriented towards cooperative and communitarian life-styles.[68] Thus, her society of hill women in the Wanderground reflects Gearhart's belief that women are natural anarchists - a belief also shared by LeGuin, who states in "Is Gender Necessary?":

> To me the "female principle" is, or at least historically has been, basically anarchic. It values order without constraint, rule by custom not by force. It has been the male who enforces order, who constructs power-structures, who makes, enforces and breaks laws.[69]

Nancy Evechild, Margot Rideau, Beverly Adams and Mary Hastings observe that feminists, because of their inclination towards non-hierarchical relationships, their preference of working in small groups, and their ability to draw advantage from the power of the masses are called *natural* anarchists.[70]

In their essay they also elaborate that anarchism must be carried by the whole society and not by an elitist leadership group, that it stresses the political nature of the personal (as does Radical Feminism), which includes an understanding of

---

[67]Cf. Nancy Evechild, Margot Rideau, Beverly Adams, Mary Hastings, "Anarcha-Feminismus - Eine Darstellung," in *Anarcha-Feminismus*, Edition Schwarze Kirschen 1 (Berlin: Libertad Verlag, 1979), p. 18. Originally published as "Anarcha-Feminism - Two Statements," *Anarchist Review*, 1,3 (1977).

[68]See Sally M. Gearhart, "Womanpower: Energy Re-Sourcement," in *The Politics of Women's Spirituality*, pp. 194-206. Originally published in *Womanspirit*, 2,7 (1976); and "The Future - If There Is One - Is Female," in *Reweaving the Web of Life*, P. McAllister, ed. (Philadelphia: New Society Publishers, 1982) pp. 268-284.

[69]LeGuin, "Is Gender Necessary?" p. 165. In the commented new edition of this essay in *Dancing at the Edge of the World*, LeGuin re-wrote this famous passage in the following way: "The 'female principle' has historically been anarchic, that is, anarchy has historically been identified as female. The domain allotted to women - 'the family,' for example - is the area of order without coercion, rule by custom not by force. Men have reserved the structures of social power to themselves (and those few women whom they admit to it on male terms, such as queens, prime ministers); men make the wars and peaces, men make, enforce, and break the laws." (pp. 11-12) Quite clearly, LeGuin does *not* share Gearhart's biologism; instead, she remains consistent in her view of mental or psychological androgyny in both sexes.

[70]Evechild *et al.*, "Anarcha-Feminismus," p. 9.

the need for festivity, play, and joy and the possibility to renew spent energies this way, that it favors cultural diversity and full personal development and that it is based on a self-created voluntary cooperation which is functional, absolutely non-hierarchic and non-coercive.[71] All of these features can be found in the society of the hill women. Gearhart's indictment of men is, however, much sharper than LeGuin's because she regards men as basically power-hungry and unwilling if not unable, to share power:

> Collectivity, I think, and women's special capacity for it, needs to be talked about elsewhere and by many of us. My own thoughts on it right now are that (1) we are uniquely *in touch with* the internal energy source; (2) we are *conscious* of what we are in touch with; and (3) we have the *intentionality to share* that energy. That makes us anarchists of sorts, whose only government is self-government. Then, I'm thinking we are uniquely capable of collectivity because we are beginning to practice . . . a new use of *inter*personal energy. We have started to look at things non-hierarchically. . . . If men have ever found an internal energy flow, and even if they have been conscious of what cosmic force they have thus tapped, they have been unable, I believe, to take the next step: intending to share that power. My continuing experience of men is that they feel they need women in order to do these things, that really respecting and loving one another, trusting one another, and dialoguing with one another are functions they cannot or will not reach out for by themselves, as men. Even the struggles of gay men toward non-power brotherhood suggest to me that collectivizing internal power may not be men's gift; . . . sharing it in non-power forms is perhaps at this time and place not a possibility for the male psyche.[72]

In Gearhart's view, men are not only unable to be loving and caring, they are also the source of violence:

> [M]alekind has seen the possible, he has consistently done the possible, he has justified his acts as manifestations of his human superiority, and he has made seem natural and right the use of force in human affairs. His assumptions have guaranteed us all of a strong and constantly proliferating civilization built upon objectification and violation. For me, the exercise of the assumptions on the part of male knowledge and male power is sufficient to indict the male of our species as the source of violence.[73]

In her essay "The Future - If There Is One - Is Female" Gearhart links maleness with the negative qualities of objectification, violence, and competitiveness whereas the female is oriented towards empathy, nurturance, and cooperation.[74] Although she concedes that present research does not yet yield definite proof whether the male is "naturally" violent and the female "naturally" nurturant, she nevertheless proposes radically reducing the ratio of men to the overall population to ten per cent, such a reduction being the only possibility to keep the violence which they alone cause at bay.[75]

---

[71]*ibid.*, pp. 11, 15-16, 18. Cf. also Lyman Tower Sargent, "A New Anarchism: Social and Political Ideas in Some Recent Feminist Eutopias," in *Women and Utopia*, Barr and Smith, eds. (Lanham *et al.*: University Press of America, 1988) pp. 3-9.

[72]Gearhart, "Womanpower," pp. 198-199.

[73]Gearhart, "The Future - If There Is One - Is Female," pp. 269-270.

[74]*ibid.*, p. 271 *et passim*.

[75]*ibid.*, pp. 270, 280-284. Gearhart emphasizes the fact that in reducing the male ratio no lives must be spent. The reduction is to be achieved slowly with the help of genetic manipulation.

Although these beliefs about men could well lead to the idea of a separatist society of women which would deliberately exclude men, this is not how the Wanderground came into existence. The hill women did not create their society voluntarily: it was male violence against women which necessitated their flight from the patriarchal city. In many cases, their lives depended on it, as we learn from the "remember rooms".

In creating an all-women society, Gearhart evokes an old myth, even an archetype, namely that of the Amazons and the Amazon state. It is not yet certain whether such states ever existed, but tales and legends about Amazons are remarkably widespread (Asia, Europe, Africa, South America).[76] In her essay "The Amazon Legacy" Phyllis Chesler states:

> We have no tangible written record of the deeds and thoughts of legendary Amazon societies. Either such records never existed or they were destroyed. Perhaps they have yet to be unearthed. What we know about Amazons comes to us only through men - and men who wrote, traveled, fought, and painted in fiercely patriarchal cultures. As such, it is remarkable that any "proof" of Amazons exists at all. What proof does exist must be viewed as a combination of phobic male denials and hasty, guilty admissions, as a somewhat distorted and suppressed record of both fact and feeling, and as an inevitably romantic confusion of matriarchal and Amazon themes.[77]

After discussing various "proofs" of Amazonism such as Hellenistic history, travelogues, and artifacts, she concludes:

> Such proofs are highly controversial and can be explained in many ways, but the geographical universality and historical longevity of the belief in legendary Amazonism is almost more important proof of their ancient existence than are various artifacts. Strong beliefs - legends that won't die - are always some sort of race-memory. The lasting belief in Amazons embodies a universal history of male-female conflict, and the Amazon myths presuppose the existence of the Great Mother cultures.[78]

Chesler puts the Amazon state in its right context: it represents a special form of matriarchal culture. As in the case of matriarchal societies it does not matter as much whether Amazons existed in history or not - they, too, have helped to strengthen modern feminists' idea of the possibility of strong and powerful women.

In Western culture the concept of Amazon women is mostly shaped by Greek mythology which pictures them as all-women states which reject and exclude men (in their most extreme form by the use of male infanticide). Amazons were excellent warriors who could face the most famous Greek heroes as equals (e.g.

---

[76]Cf. Phyllis Chesler, "The Amazon Legacy," in *The Politics of Women's Spirituality*, pp. 97-113. Excerpted from "The Amazon Legacy: An Interpretive Essay," *Wonder Woman, Ms.* (New York et al.: Holt, Rinehart and Winston, 1972.)
[77]*ibid.*, p. 98.
[78]*ibid.*, p. 99.

Hippolyte-Hercules/Theseus, Penthesilea-Achilles) although, in the end, they always had to yield to patriarchal power.

Chesler observes that "Amazons are a universal male nightmare, exorcised by ridicule or disbelief."[79] Seemingly the idea of strong and independent women arouses fear and rejection in a patriarchal culture in which they must necessarily appear dangerous and subversive. These feelings must be heightened by the fact that Amazons exclude men - not so much because they hate men but because they just do not care to live with them. The latter is regarded as the deepest affront in a patriarchal culture.[80] The belligerence of Amazons only flares up in cases in which they are attacked by patriarchal forces and have to defend themselves and their matriarchal values or rescue one of their sisters from patriarchal subjugation (e.g. Antiope-Theseus).

In the context of the contemporary Women's Movement the Amazon myth has been taken up by lesbian women:

> The development of utopian ideas from sociohistorical subject matter, not on the level of social discourse, but in the everyday praxis of women, who consciously create a new life style and who profess to it openly, is for example characteristic of the movement of Lesbianism within the Women's Movement. For them, Amazon states often serve . . . as models of a pre-patriarchal social form in which female homosexual love, with the social and even the physical exclusion of men, dominated.[81]

Mythical Amazon warriors aggressively opposed the threat of violent patriarchal conquest. Today, this opposition has taken a different form: "[the fight] is the total rejection of the other sex, connected with individual as well as social separatism."[82] This is what the hill women are doing, and it is the politics of Lesbian Separatism as a special form of Radical Feminism which Gearhart endorses in her essays and in her novel as well.

The core of Radical Feminism holds that male supremacy and the subjugation of women constitute the model oppression in society.[83] Contrary to Socialist or Marxist Feminism it postulates that patriarchy, not capitalism, is the root of women's oppression. It is therefore necessary for women to identify themselves as an oppressed political class. Radical Feminism must be the basis for any truly revolutionary change. It further claims that the personal is political, thus attacking such seemingly "private" institutions as marriage, family, and traditional sexuality, and that women should put their primary energies into the Women's Movement in order to fight the oppressor. In its elaboration of the fundamental difference in style and culture between men and women Radical Feminism follows its nineteenth century predecessor, Cultural Feminism. This difference between the sexes causes problems in the theory: Most Cultural Feminists regarded it as a difference in nature and determined by biology (e.g. Margaret Fuller) whereas theorists like Gilman considered the difference to be social, its characteristics to be capable of change, leading to an androgynous idea of

---

[79]*ibid.*, p. 95.

[80]Joanna Russ called this the "taboo against being indifferent to The Man." "Reflections in Science Fiction - An Interview with Joanna Russ," in *Building Feminist Theory: Essays from QUEST* (New York, London: Longman, 1981) p. 243.

[81]Göttner-Abendroth, "Der unversöhnliche Traum," p. 12. Author's translation.

[82]*ibid.* Author's translation.

[83]For the following discussion of Radical, Cultural, and Lesbian Feminism, see Donovan, *Feminist Theory*, chapters 2 and 6.

56

humanity. Radical Feminism faces the same problems but, although important theorists such as Shulamith Firestone in her pioneer work *The Dialectics of Sex* (1970) base their analysis on biological determinism, most Radical Feminists reject this and derive women's oppression from social conditioning instead. In their view women need to define their own mode which then ought to become the basis for any future society.

* * *

In the course of the seventies lesbian feminists began to address themselves to the problem of their oppression due to gender and homosexuality - the latter even within the Women's Movement itself. They focused on "heterosexualism" (compulsory heterosexuality as a political institution). Woman-to-woman-relationships became the model egalitarian bond as they precluded sex-roles and enabled women to adopt a new life-style which was not "male-identified," i.e. free from standards defined by patriarchal culture. In its most radical form Lesbian Feminism calls for women to separate from men in order to formulate the utopia of an all-women's culture. This cultural separatism is also pacifist, demands an ecologically holistic vision and often also requires vegetarianism because it perceives a connection between carnivorism and sexism due to a pre-historic role-division according to which men hunted, killed, and ate meat.

Obviously, Gearhart espouses the tenets of Lesbian Feminism as well as the biological determinism inherited from Cultural Feminism. The mythical Amazon state thus serves as a model for her utopian design of an all-women society, but the patriarchal "nightmarish" woman warrior is transformed into the peace-loving cultural separatist described above. As mentioned before, the hill women did not deliberately separate from the society of the city but were forced to do so by male violence. As Chesler found out, the mythical Amazon is often seen in the context of a gender conflict as she is forced to defend the Great Mother culture against patriarchal conquest. The "nightmarish" Amazon is therefore a reaction to and a product of patriarchy itself.

In *The Wanderground*, this is dramatized in the form of the armored stranger in the opening story, the raped woman. June Howard observes: "the story suggests that the violence done to women damages and changes us, forces us to become hardened against it and thus to dress in armor though underneath we are wounded."[84] The "real" Amazons, i.e. those who are not seen in a distorted way through patriarchal bias, are the strong, independent, and self-sufficient women of the Wanderground, who, because of their strength and the full development of their abilities, have no need to hate men: Being truly independent, they are even free from that last condition which is the other side of dependence on and definition by men, namely the attempted negation of this society by rebellion against it. The hill women have transcended this dialectic with the creation of their feminocentric society - although it is endangered again and they have to be on guard.

In *The Wanderground*, the Amazonian imagery and its connection to the theory of Lesbian Feminism and Cultural Separatism form only one aspect of the utopian society. The strong Amazon woman, willing and able to protect her realm, is also the matriarchal witch who has reclaimed what is often termed 'ancient female knowledge'. This includes the reliance on symbols traditionally associated with the feminine (e.g. the moon), the re-interpretation and

---

[84]Howard, "Widening the Dialogue," p. 68.

transformation of old myth (as for instance the re-telling of the Demeter-Kore myth, *The Wanderground*, pp. 74-76), witchcraft, and the occult.

The image of the witch, which in fairy-tales has degenerated into the evil old woman, is also positively transformed. Thus, in episodes where women are depicted as practicing witchcraft (e.g. healing with blood and earth in "Sisterblood", pp. 33-42, "windriding" = flying in "Windriding", pp. 102-109, and "Meeting the Gentles", pp. 167-181 - here even in the company of crows, true "accessoires" of fairy-tale witches) the negative images are subverted in a playful way by the use of humor or, in the case of healing, they show the woman in a serious way as compassionate and not too powerful, i.e. she depends on nature. There is nothing terrifying about Gearhart's witches.

The emphasis on the political importance of the practice of witchcraft and occult techniques leads to the special theory of Spiritual Feminism, which is the most important theory for Gearhart. She is a feminist activist who is also active in the gay liberation and animal rights movements. So far, she has written only one piece of fiction, namely *The Wanderground*, otherwise she expresses herself in political essays. Her article "Womanpower: Energy Re-Sourcement" (1976) can almost be read as a non-fictional blueprint for *The Wanderground* - or, conversely, *The Wanderground* can be regarded as the fictional realization of the politics Gearhart believes in. In "Womanpower" she rejects the usual strategies of feminist activism which she defines as a) revolutionary actions against the system, radical political organizing; b) seizing power within the system through consciously chosen reforms and c) the creation of alternative organizations or structures.[85] In her opinion, these are not powerful enough to beat the patriarchy but they act as a sort of protective buffer zone for the fourth strategy which Gearhart calls "re-sourcement":

> What I am calling re-sourcement is the activity of women who are reaching out for new ways of understanding and viewing reality, i.e. *they are articulating a new epistemology*: astrology, the Tarot, numerology, the I Ching, the Kabbala - all these and others reinterpreted and/or redeemed from their masculist emphases and filtered anew through the channels of womanknowing, womansight. [86]

This source is "deeper than the patriarchy" and allows women "to stand in the path of continuous and cosmic energy."[87] This is an *intra*personal energy which must be found within the self, then it may become the basis for *inter*personal energy which is the kind of energy which flows between people. "What we have experienced with the patriarchy," Gearhart writes, "is *inter*personal energy which has not first been founded on, which has never been connected to, *intra*personal energy."[88] This use of interpersonal energy is destructive and leads to power-over-relationships.[89] Gearhart believes that re-sourcement will be "womanpower" because women seem to possess a unique capacity for collective functioning and internal sourcing.[90] It will also bring about a new ethic and a new value system which will allow women to reclaim their bodies and ancient healing methods as well as to relate to "the Earth Herself and the healing of Her ten-thousand-year-

---

[85] Gearhart, "Womanpower," pp. 194-195.
[86] *ibid.*, p. 195.
[87] *ibid.*
[88] *ibid.*
[89] *ibid.*, p. 196.
[90] *ibid.*, p. 197.

long-rape," to animals and plants and also to connect to the biosphere.[91] These beliefs account for the metaphysical skills of the Wanderground women, the use of telepathy even with animals, plants and the "Earth Herself" (water, clouds, moon).

As she perceives our patriarchal culture to be filled with destructive interpersonal energy patterns, she perceives for women "*the need for separatism: the separation of women from the patriarchal system in quantities great enough to make a qualitative difference in history.*"[92] Because it is a movement of women only, it has "a *strong and unashamed lesbian component.*"[93] In this respect, *The Wanderground* is the utopian dream vision of Gearhart's political beliefs. The women's mental skills, which lead to an entirely new and loving mode of interaction among themselves as well as between themselves and nature (Lefanu speaks of "a vision *par excellence* of the unity of mind and body")[94], and the anarchic organization of the Wanderground society exemplify the fact that Gearhart's political activism is informed by a concretely imagined utopia in the same way as is Piercy's *Woman on the Edge of Time.* This shows once more the close relationship between utopia and politics.

The Wanderground, however, does not really qualify as a utopia because many aspects of the organization of the Wanderground society are not sufficiently explained. We learn that children are conceived parthenogenetically (ovular merging, presumably with the help of plants) and that they have seven mothers, the "Pleiad", in order to break the nuclear bond, but we are not informed about the actual child-rearing and educational system. We know that the women have to perform work and tasks such as guards, "remember-guides", going on "rotation" in the city and so on, but we are not told how these tasks are distributed. Lefanu observes correctly:

> [O]verall there is no sense of the materiality of the women's lives. Unlike the societies depicted by Marge Piercy . . ., questions about food, clothing, building materials are left vague. . . . Yet perhaps it is not so strange, for the elements of realism in this book are confined, like the men, to the City, where there is an attempt, even if only sketchy, to show the history of a social and political process . . . The Wanderground is a *dream world*, a world with its past named only through what it has rejected, a world without history or future, a world in which the questions 'how?' or 'by what process?' are irrelevant.[95]

Still, there is an emphasis on the good of the Wanderground society. It is meant to describe a better world for women. *The Wanderground* is obviously didactic about this; the reader is often confronted with sayings such as "There are no words more obscene than 'I can't live without you.' Count them the deepest affront to the person" (*The Wanderground*, p. 3), in order to learn the rules of this better world.

* * *

---

[91]*ibid.*, p. 196.
[92]*ibid.*, p. 197.
[93]*ibid.*, p. 203.
[94]Lefanu, *In the Chinks of the World Machine*, p. 66.
[95]*ibid.*, p. 67. Emphasis added.

Whether *The Wanderground* can be considered a "dream world" depends also largely on the reader's attitude towards the credibility of the women's metaphysical skills. Parapsychologists and mystics might well consider them possible, and so does Gearhart. As her use of parapsychology and esoterics is consistent and oriented towards whatever scientific results are yielded by these disciplines, Gearhart's novel should be classified as science fiction. More specifically, *The Wanderground* may be regarded as a critical utopia according to Moylan (see 1.2) because the Wanderground is a fictitious utopian society in conflict with its simultaneously existing parent society, the city. Both of these worlds are related to our own - the city being a dystopian extrapolation and the Wanderground a utopian hope.

* * *

The evaluation of *The Wanderground* is even more difficult than its literary classification. Gearhart defies the prevalent attitude towards parapsychology and esoterics (i.e. not to take it seriously, even to ridicule it) in her serious and over-extensive use of it. The readers' own attitude towards these fields will influence them in their evaluation (or even classification) of *The Wanderground*.

Even more provocative are the openly endorsed politics of the book. "*The Wanderground* is, I think, a difficult book for men to read, since it appears to stress only feminist separatism," says Lefanu.[96] For the same reasons, many women may be expected to resent *The Wanderground*. The politics of the book are highly controversial among feminists - a fact which Gearhart anticipated in her essay "Womanpower". The debate about biological determinism has already been mentioned. The assumption of a natural difference of the sexes runs counter to a critique of social circumstances and the belief in their mutability.[97] Howard criticizes in particular Gearhart's implicit opinion that feminist activism is ineffective, that women are essentially powerless in a man's world (city), and that the only solution seems to be escape. She is most disturbed by the fact that in *The Wanderground*, the salvation is not brought about by the efforts of women but by the miraculous intervention of the "Revolt of the Earth": a "*dea ex machina*."[98] Although I personally consider this criticism of politics to be valid, I want to point out once more that Gearhart's politics are just as serious and theoretically consistent as any other feminist politics if one does not reject parapsychological phenomena outright. Howard's criticism is related to political opinions and not to literary aspects, a phenomenon quite common in feminist criticism of feminist literature. It remains only to add that the concept of the "Revolt of the Earth" is indeed part of present-day mysticism:

> The longer this massacre of Earth and Air lasts, the stronger the reaction will be, when the Earth cleanses itself.
>
> This unison of cosmic rays must occur, because otherwise the end of the Earth would be inevitable. In that moment, however, in which by its own efforts, it finds its balance again, it will cleanse itself according to its own idea and not according to ours.[99]

---

[96]*ibid.*, p. 69.
[97]Howard, "Widening the Dialogue," p. 72.
[98]*ibid.*, p. 74.
[99]Lisa Malin, *Die schönen Kräfte: Eine Arbeit über Heilen in verschiedenen Dimensionen* (Frankfurt a.M.: Zweitausendeins, 1986) p. 115. Originally accepted as dissertation at the University of Vienna

Lefanu's reading of *The Wanderground* suggests a possible positive interpretation in terms of presenting a powerful image on the psychological level:

> In many ways the novel represents an imaginative recreation of an unthreatening childhood world, one that exists before the complexities and dangers of language and sexuality come into being . . . . *The Wanderground* takes us back to an earlier self, ignorant of the strictures and limitations concomitant with being female in a male-dominated world, a self whose imagination and desire are strong enough and clear enough to create a vision of an 'if only . . .' world that sweeps aside those limitations and explores instead the endless realm of potential.[100]

Apart from these discussions of the content of *The Wanderground*, it remains to be stated that it is an aesthetically flawed book. Its tone is overly pathetic, and Gearhart indulges excessively in sentimental romanticism. In her view of a past oriented society without technology the simple life in nature is unrealistically idealized, thus undermining the utopian intention. The use of metaphysical phenomena and the language invented for them ask too much of the reader's imagination. Gearhart did, however, manage to handle the didactics of the book better than Piercy in using narrative devices similar to LeGuin (e.g. historical archives of the "remember rooms", use of myth in order to explain ethics and morals).

* * *

Let me conclude this discussion of *The Wanderground* with a survey of its literary predecessors. In part 1.3 some early fictional all-women societies were already mentioned. The increase in the number of women writers using science fiction and utopia to portray better worlds for women has also entailed an increase in the number of novels about all-women societies. Among the most noteworthy are the peaceful Whileaway in Joanna Russ's *The Female Man* (1975) and Suzy McKee Charnas' *Walk to the End of the World* (1974) and *Motherlines* (1979). Monique Wittig's *Les Guérillères* (1969), published in the U.S.A. in 1973, is an important predecessor, too. Wittig's Amazon women are literally at war with the patriarchy. She is the first to have used a true cluster-protagonist in the line of all-women societies, i.e. the whole society is the protagonist and no single woman 'stars' in the story. She also anticipated many themes of later all-women societies (e.g. the importance of rituals and celebrations or the stigmatization of male violence).

The novella *Consider Her Ways* (1956) by John Wyndham should be mentioned as an interesting contribution by a male author. Wyndham's future all-women society is benevolent and orderly but sterile and resembling Huxley's *Brave New World* in the creation of physically different classes of women for different tasks such as bearing children or road construction. The future historian Laura delivers an accurate and compassionate analysis of the sexism of the author's time, yet his design of a possible women's world is ambiguous and not all favorable, and certainly not an ideal to be striven for.

The most important difference between the nineteenth-century women's worlds of Gilman and Lane and also *Consider Her Ways*, and their modern

---

under the title "Die Aporetik des Heilens." Author's translation. Gearhart refers to many mystic beliefs which are explained in this book.
[100]Lefanu, *In the Chinks of the World Machine*, p. 69.

successors is the open inclusion of lesbianism in the latter. Keinhorst explains the lack of sexuality in the former:

> This must be understood in the context of the time when the institution of heterosexuality relegated all sexuality to the realm of marriage and declared lesbian sexuality to be non-existent. Moreover, a sexuality wholly dictated by men, which often was not sensually gratifying because it was not self-determined and fertility-bound, was not necessarily considered a loss, and could simply be omitted for the convenience of contemporary women readers.[101]

Tucker Farley remarks that in the nineteenth century lesbianism did not need to be overtly mentioned because all kinds of relationships between women were allowed - even if only tacitly.[102] The idea of lesbian love does not seem to occur to Wyndham at all because the most deplorable flaw of his all-women society is the (seeming) impossibility of romance. The lesbianism in contemporary women's writing is to be seen in the context of the modern feminist movement and Lesbian Feminism.

Although Gearhart is serious about separatism and mysticism, her novel *The Wanderground* with its dream-like qualities is probably meant as a thought-experiment accompanied by some wishful thinking. Joanna Russ sums up the most important implications of separatist utopian designs in the following statement:

> I am not a separatist in the sense that I envision the perfect future for our planet as a manless one - such an eventuality seems to me undesirable, immoral and totally impossible - but *I do believe that crucial to the process of women becoming primary to themselves is the possibility of becoming able to imagine such a state.* . . . And the all-female, feminist Utopias provide explicit and clearly stated reasons for keeping men out: rape, battery, the threats thereof that restrict women's freedom and safety, and the male monopoly of activity in the public world. (The resemblance to our world is not coincidental.)[103]

---

[101]Keinhorst, *Utopien von Frauen*, p. 123. Author's translation.

[102]Tucker Farley, "Realities and Fictions: Lesbian Visions of Utopia," in *Women in Search of Utopia*, p. 236. Cf. also Donovan, *Feminist Theory*, on Cultural Feminists, pp. 53-54.

[103]Joanna Russ, "Letter," *Science Fiction Studies*, 7 (1980) p. 235. Emphasis added.

3. COMPARISON OF SPECIAL ASPECTS OF THE SOCIETIES DEPICTED IN *THE LEFT HAND OF DARKNESS, WOMAN ON THE EDGE OF TIME*, AND *THE WANDERGROUND*

The discussions of *The Left Hand of Darkness, Woman on the Edge of Time*, and *The Wanderground* have shown that the designs of societies described in them are very different. It is, however, the similarities of these very different societies that I wish to discuss - but I shall also consider the differences and the reasons for them, which can be traced to different ideologies and politics. I find these differences important because most feminist critics tend to overemphasize the similarities and level out the differences in order to support their own feminist beliefs.[1]
As there exists no unified feminist theory, a closer look at various conceptions of alternative societies and the way in which they are conceived and conveyed will reveal interesting variations in the respective authors' own beliefs and opinions. The following section deals with four exemplary areas for comparison: the personal realm, the public realm, religion and mysticism, and language.

3.1 The Personal Realm: Sex/Gender Roles, Relationships

The imaginative societies of *The Left Hand of Darkness, Woman on the Edge of Time*, and *The Wanderground* all imply a critique of contemporary stereotypical gender roles. Due to the differences in the societies, these critiques take different forms, too.
The hermaphrodites of *The Left Hand of Darkness* are metaphors for what LeGuin perceives to be an already existing psychological gender equality. The Gethenians' hermaphroditism, however, has specific physiological consequences:

> The sexual cycle averages 26 to 28 days (. . . .) For 21 or 22 days the individual is *somer*, sexually inactive, latent. On about the 18th day hormonal changes are initiated by the pituitary control and on the 22nd or 23rd day the individual enters *kemmer*, estrus. In the first phase of kemmer (karh. *secher*) he remains completely androgynous. Gender, and potency, are not attained in isolation. A Gethenian in first-phase kemmer, if kept alone or with others not in kemmer, remains incapable of coitus. Yet the sexual impulse is tremendously strong in this phase, controlling the entire personality, subjecting all other drives to its imperative. When the individual finds a partner in kemmer, hormonal secretion is further stimulated . . . until in one partner either a male or female hormonal dominance is established . . . . Normal individuals have no predisposition to either sexual role in kemmer; they do not know

---

[1]The examples are too numerous to list. One of them is Sally M. Gearhart's "Future Visions: Today's Politics: Feminist Utopias in Review," in *Women in Search of Utopia*, pp. 296-309. She here requires feminist utopias to present men or male institutions as "a major cause of present social ills" and women as "sole arbiters of their reproductive functions." (p. 296)

whether they will be the male or the female, and have no choice in the matter. (*The Left Hand of Darkness*, pp. 62-63)

After two to five days of sexual capacity the Gethenians return to their androgynous state. If conception takes place, the respective Gethenian will remain female during the ensuing gestation and lactation periods before returning to the previous latent, androgynous state. The investigator Ong Tot Oppong adds that even after having given birth, "[n]o physiological habit is established, and the mother of several children may be the father of several more." (*The Left Hand of Darkness*, pp. 63-64) One very important physiological consequence of this biology is the impossibility of rape: "As with most mammals other than man, coitus can be performed only by mutual invitation and consent; otherwise it is not possible."(*The Left Hand of Darkness*, p. 65) This is of considerable social consequence. Aggression in the sexual sphere is furthermore unlikely because

> the limitation of the sexual drive to a discontinuous time-segment, and the "equalizing" of it in androgyny, must prevent, to a large extent, both the exploitation and the frustration of the drive. There must be sexual frustration (though society provides as well as it can against it; so long as the social unit is large enough that more than one person will be in kemmer at one time, sexual fulfillment is fairly certain), but at least it cannot build up; it is over when kemmer is over. (*The Left Hand of Darkness*, p. 66)

On the sociological plane, the fact that every Gethenian may have children is very important. Ong Tot Oppong remarks:

> Anyone can turn his hand on anything . . . . The fact that everyone between seventeen and thirty-five or so is liable to be (. . .) "tied down to childbearing," implies that no one is quite so thoroughly "tied down" here as women, elsewhere, are likely to be - psychologically or physically. Burden and privilege are shared out pretty equally; everybody has the same risk to run or choice to make. Therefore nobody here is quite so free as a free male anywhere else. (*The Left Hand of Darkness*, p. 65)

This discussion of the effect of motherhood in an androgynous society clearly criticizes the institution of motherhood in our own culture as a means of restricting women to this one role and of denying them full participation in public life. Women are expected to see their primary task in the raising of their children and have to carry that responsibility alone, whereas the role of the father requires him to spend his time in the public area in order to provide for his family in material terms. LeGuin proposed a different model in *The Left Hand of Darkness*. On Gethen, the descent is reckoned by the "mother-of-the-flesh", i.e. the parent who actually bears the child. This is the same as matrilinear descent. Although the other parent takes an interest in the child, he is not responsible for it because it will stay in the "mother's" clan. This does not mean, however, that the "mother" is solely responsible for her child. Genly Ai observes:

> A quarter to a third of the urban population is engaged full time in the nurture and education of the children. Here [i.e. in rural Karhide] the clan looked after its own; nobody and everybody was responsible for them." (*The Left Hand of Darkness*, p. 69)

64

In the case of Estraven and his own "child-of-the-flesh", we learn that it is possible to leave one's child behind in the clan who will then look after it if one decides to leave the Hearth (the community of the clan). The Gethenians' readiness to attend to all children and the importance they place on extensive child-care might be further explained by another observation made by Genly Ai:

> Their tenderness toward their children struck me as being profound, effective, and almost wholly unpossessive. Only in that unpossessivemess does it perhaps differ from what we call the "maternal" instinct. I suspect that the disctinction between a maternal and a paternal instinct is scarcely worth making; the parental instinct, the wish to protect, to further, is not a sex-linked characteristic . . . . (*The Left Hand of Darkness*, p. 69)

Genly Ai, the representative from Earth, i.e. from our culture, seems to regard this Gethenian arrangement as an ideal.

In our culture, possessiveness towards children is characteristic of both sexes but manifests itself differently and has different causes for men and women.

According to the Radical Feminist analysis, a patriarchal culture requires men to produce heirs; women are expected to fulfill their role as mothers. Shulamith Firestone, for instance, perceives an

> attempted extension of ego through one's children - in the case of the man, the "immortalization" of name, property, class, and ethnic identification, and in the case of the woman, motherhood as the justification of her existence.[2]

She further hypothesizes:

> Perhaps when we strip parenthood of these other functions, we will find a real instinct for parenthood even on the part of men, a simple physical desire to associate with the young.[3]

The Gethenian hermaphrodites have no need to project such functions (regarded as sex-linked phenomena obscuring a purer parental instinct by both LeGuin and Firestone) onto their children.

Possessiveness towards children precludes a communal interest in and a sharing of responsibility for children in a larger societal unit. Thus, sex-roles which define constructs such as "motherhood" and "fatherhood" may be seen as restricting personal development and also as potentially detrimental to children, who become objects in their parents' ego-establishments. Furthermore, these sex-roles and the ensuing "privatization" of children prevent society as a whole from providing better child-care since it does not feel responsible for its children.

Although LeGuin raised the point of sex-role defined motherhood in her novel, hinting at the underlying implications, she did not fully develop it. Apart from mentioning that a very large number of Gethenians is involved in the care of children, LeGuin neither made an effort to describe the child-care system in any detail, nor did she show us a "mothering" Gethenian. She has been much criticized because of this.[4] She herself admits that she neglected to show

---

[2]Shulamith Firestone, *The Dialectic of Sex: The Case for Feminist Revolution* (New York: Bantam, 1970) p. 229.
[3]*ibid.*, p. 230.
[4]See, for instance, Russ, "The Image of Women in Science Fiction," p. 39.

the "female" component of Gethenian characters in *action*. Unfortunately, the plot and structure that arose as I worked the book out cast the Gethenian protagonist, Estraven, almost exclusively into roles which we are culturally conditioned to perceive as "male" - a prime minister (it takes more than even Golda Meir and Indira Gandhi to break a stereotype), a political schemer, a fugitive, a prisonbreaker, a sledge-hauler .... One does not see Estraven as a mother, with his children, in any role which we automatically perceive as "female": and therefore, we tend to see him as a man. This is a real flaw in the book.[5]

LeGuin occasionally attempts to stun the readers' expectations about gender stereotypes - for instance, when Genly Ai thinks of the superintendent of his living quarters as being feminine:

> I thought of him as my landlady, for he had fat buttocks that wagged as he walked, and a soft fat face, and a prying, spying, ignoble, kindly nature .... He was so feminine in looks and manner that I once asked him how many children he had. He looked glum. He had never borne any. He had, however, sired four. (*The Left Hand of Darkness*, pp. 33-34)

More often, however, LeGuin is trapped by what Russ calls "traditional assumptions which are nothing more than traditional straitjackets."[6] So Faxe the Weaver turns into a woman during the ritual Foretelling, evoking the cliché of woman as prophetess or witch. Gaum, an agent of the SARF, the Orgota secret service, when trying to seduce Estraven, turns into a woman, thus conforming to one of the most common sex-role clichés for women: the evil seductress. Estraven is shown as a masculine contrast once more in comparison to his former "kemmering" (spouse) Ashe, who is clearly feminine in being "long-suffering, mild, and gentle."[7]

Omitting to show the female/feminine side in Estraven - and in the Gethenians in general - has led to criticism of LeGuin's use of the androgyne. Jewell Parker Rhodes, for instance, claims that the myths of androgyny in our culture have favored the male completion model, i.e. the completion of positive qualities associated with masculinity/maleness by positive feminine/female traits, but not vice versa. She criticizes the fact that the notion of androgyny does not allow the view of men and women as complete unto themselves; instead, sexual polarity is reinforced in the concept of androgyny as mutual completion. It is therefore unfit to symbolize the transcendence of gender. Moreover, she rejects androgyny because it is based on heterosexuality as the norm. Gethenian "kemmering" is, in her opinion, "a variation of the romantic theme of androgyny; heterosexual sex restores primordial unity."[8] LeGuin herself admitts that she

---

[5]LeGuin, "Is Gender Necessary?", p. 168. In the new edition of "Is Gender Necessary?" LeGuin comments the latter part of this passage thus: "One does not see Estraven as a mother, with his children [strike 'his'], in any role which we automatically perceive as 'female': and therefore we tend to see him as a man [place 'him' in quotation marks, please]. This is a real flaw in the book." (p. 15)
[6]Russ, "The Image of Women in Science Fiction," p. 39.
[7]*ibid.*
[8]Jewell Parker Rhodes, "Ursula LeGuin's *The Left Hand of Darkness*: Androgyny and the Feminist Utopia," in *Women and Utopia: Critical Interpretations*, p. 116. pp. 108-120. Cf. also Gisela Ecker, "The Politics of Fantasy," p. 506. For a discussion of androgyny as male completion model in our culture, see two articles in *Frauen - Weiblichkeit - Schrift*, R. Berger *et al.*, ed. (Berlin: Argument,

quite unnecessarily locked the Gethenians into heterosexuality. It is a naively pragmatic view of sex that insists that sexual partners must be of opposite sex! In any kemmerhouse homosexual practice would, of course, be possible and acceptable and welcomed - but I never thought to explore this option; and the omission, alas, implies that sexuality is heterosexuality. I regret this very much.[9]

Obviously LeGuin does not consider androgyny and heterosexuality to be linked in the way Rhodes does. To her, the concept of androgyny is a psychological (rather than a biological) one, referring to feminine and masculine (rather than to female and male) aspects, which are culturally and socially determined. Thus one can argue that androgyny, in LeGuin's view, would not be a completion but a neutralization - and ultimately an abolition - of "feminine" and "masculine".[10] Nor is Gethenian sexuality determined by completion or a need for "the Other". There is, however, a need to explain reproduction on Gethen in an inherently logical way.

* * *

The attempted portrayal of a gender-free society in *The Left Hand of Darkness* remains largely theoretical, as for example in the musings of Ong Tot Oppong:

> There is no division of humanity into strong and weak halves, protective/protected, dominant/submissive, owner/chattel, active/passive. In fact the whole tendency to dualism that pervades human thinking may be found to be lessened, or changed, on Winter . . . .
> When you meet a Gethenian you cannot and must not do what a bisexual naturally does, which is to cast him in the role of Man or Woman, while adopting towards him a corresponding role dependent of your expectations of the patterned or possible interactions between persons of the same or the opposite sex. Our entire pattern of socio-sexual interaction is nonexistent here. (*The Left Hand of Darkness*, p. 65)

This must lead to difficulties for a gender-determined mind:

> A man wants his virility regarded, a woman wants her femininity appreciated, however indirect and subtle the indications of regard and appreciation. On Winter they will not exist. One is respected and judged only as a human being. It is an appalling experience. (*The Left Hand of Darkness*, p. 66)

Consequently, Genly Ai and Estraven have problems with their communication. Genly Ai's virility, for instance, does not allow him to cry, whereas Gethenians cry easily and are generally very emotional people. Their social interactions are not determined by gender roles but by *shifgrethor*, which is

---

1985): Susanne Amrain, "Der Androgyn. Das poetische Geschlecht und sein Aktus," pp. 119-129; Hannelore Gauster, "Zur Hermaphroditen-Darstellung in der Antike," pp. 79-98.
[9]LeGuin, *Dancing at the Edge of the World*, p. 14.
[10]Rhodes' critique of the term "androgyny" - once denoting a feminist ideal but since fallen into disgrace - is very likely part of a more or less unnecessary quarrel about it among feminists today. Suggested alternatives for the concept intended include "bisexuality" (French Feminism) and "integrity". For a short review of the feminist quarrel about "androgyny", see Carolyn Heilbrun, "Androgyny and the Psychology of Sex Differences," in *The Future of Difference*, Eisenstein and Jardine, ed. (Boston: Barnard College Women's Center, G.K. Hall, 1980) pp. 258-266.

related to Chinese face-saving.[11] This highly stylized form of interaction functions on the basis of equality of the involved persons; condescending behavior is therefore avoided, for instance one does not give pieces of advice openly. For this kind of behavior, the Hopi Indians are an anthropological precedent: "Hopi are quick to criticize but hesitate to give advice because a person must always take responsibility for the consequences."[12]

This elimination of gender and its consequences, however, does not resolve all of our culture's present problems into a peaceful utopia: there still are aggression, intrigue, a hunger for power, murder, feuds, and forays. There has not yet been a war on Gethen, but Karhide and Orgoreyn come close to one. LeGuin comments her vision of Gethenian society:

> If we were socially ambisexual, if men and women were completely and genuinely equal in their social roles, equal legally and economically, equal in freedom, in responsibility, and in self-esteem, then society would be a very different thing. What our problems might be, God knows: I only know we would have them. But it seems likely that our central problem would not be the one it is now: the problem of exploitation - exploitation of the woman, of the weak, of the earth .... The dualism of value that destroys us, the dualism of superior/inferior, ruler/ruled, . . ., might give way to what seems to me, from here, a much healthier, sounder, more promising modality of integration and integrity.[13]

* * *

Whereas LeGuin, using a hermaphroditic biology as metaphor for social gender equality, does not arrive at a utopia once sex/gender are excluded, but relegates some negative phenomena such as aggressiveness and competitiveness (particularly in the social realm, in a striving for power) to human nature, shared by both sexes, Piercy seems to believe that gender equality will result in a "feminization" of society, i.e. traits and values which are regarded as feminine and subordinate in our patriarchal culture will permeate society and turn it into a utopia. LeGuin's belief in the 'human-ness' of aggressiveness and competition is probably rooted in her knowledge of anthropology, which considers these traits to be natural and necessary for survival and draws analogies between animals and between various human societies (historical and contemporary). Only when the balance is tipped and the male dominates, will natural aggression be destructive. Piercy, however, arrives at the conclusion that when gender roles are fused into an androgynous synthesis, aggression and power-hunger will no longer be necessary. This is in accord with the Radical Feminist analysis that sexual oppression constitutes a blueprint for all oppression. Once it has been overcome, there will no longer be any need to compete for power because there won't be anyone left to exert power over. Whatever drive to compete is inherent in people is channelled into sublimation such as sport. Luciente points out a young gymnast who won a first prize during a festival to Connie. Connie exclaims: "So you do have sports. You said you taught kids not to compete," but she is told:

[11]Barbara Bucknall, "Androgynes in Outer Space," in *Critical Encounters: Writers and Themes in Science Fiction*, D. Riley, ed. (New York: Ungar, 1978) p. 62.
[12]Diane LeBow, "Rethinking Matriliny Among the Hopi," in *Women in Search of Utopia*, p. 13,
[13]LeGuin, "Is Gender Necessary?" p. 169.

But try to do things well! That's fun . . . . A child playing alone will try to jump higher than that child jumped yesterday, no? We don't keep back from saluting each other for doing well. We want each other to feel . . . cherished? It's a point of emphasis, no? Maybe always some cooperating, some competing goes on. Instead of competing for a living, for scarce resources, for food, we try to cooperate on all that. Competing is like . . . decoration. Something that belongs to sports, games, fighting, wrestling, running, racing, poemfests, carnival . . . (*Woman on the Edge of Time*, pp. 174-175)

Although Piercy is able to imagine a utopia which she considers possible - and for which, consequently, no extensive metaphor such as hermaphroditism is needed - she finds it necessary to search for a remedy in the change of human biology. As in LeGuin's *The Left Hand of Darkness*, the patriarchal construct of motherhood as the predominant sex/gender role for women is singled out as the root of gender inequality. Unfortunately neither writer elaborates thoroughly on this mixing of biological factors and sociological phenomena. In LeGuin's case this is not as serious a gap because she uses Gethenian biology as a metaphor for psychological equality. She is, however, against "genetic alteration of the human organism."[14] In *Woman on the Edge of Time*, on the other hand, the gap is more obvious because Piercy is serious about her proposal of extracorporeal reproduction. So, when Piercy has Luciente claim that women's ability to give birth is a *power* which they have to give up in order to achieve sexual equality, she unfortunately omits to explain both its essence and mechanism. (*Woman on the Edge of Time*, p. 105) Apart from the fact that women are physiologically affected by pregnancy and lactation, child-raising and child-care are social factors for which a variety of systems could be devised. Piercy's own model is communal: every child is assigned three "mothers" ("coms") to whom it is not biologically or genetically related. Nevertheless children grow up together in a special children's house with expert staff (as in Gethenian cities, and as in Gilman's *Herland*), and they are relatively free to move around and associate with whomever they want. Thus the responsibility for children is basically carried by the whole society, and mothering is a service the individual performs for the society and for the child (for whom she or he is not an authoritarian guide but a helper to turn to if needed). Therefore people are not possessive towards children, who are regarded as belonging to everybody, to the whole society. This relieves the "coms". At a festival, for instance, children are allowed to stay up and participate as long as they wish. Luciente tells Connie:

"When they can't stay awake, they fall asleep. If they doze off in the grass, someone will carry them home."
"You have wonderful faith in other people!"
"Without that social faith, what a burden it would be to have children! The children are everyone's heirs, everyone's business, everyone's future."
(*Woman on the Edge of Time*, p. 183)

Around puberty the children are released into adulthood with a *rite de passage*, but even before this event they participate more fully in the public life of their village than children in our culture are allowed to.

In my opinion one might well ask why this model requires the circumvention of human biology. When Piercy intends to break the "nuclear bonding" (*Woman*

---

[14]*ibid.*, p. 163.

on the Edge of Time, p. 105) she does not explain on what it is based in the first place. Obviously it is not imperative for child and biological mother to stay together. If the bond is psychological, it may be asked that when all other psychological gender-constructs can be overcome, why shoud that this one not also be transcended? Gilman's model in *Herland* is similar to Piercy's without eliminating natural childbirth.

* * *

The politics in Piercy's novel resemble those of Firestone's *The Dialectic of Sex* very closely. In Firestone's view

> women, biologically distinguished from men, are culturally distinguished from "human". Nature produced the fundamental inequality - half the human race must bear and rear the children of all of them - which was later consolidated, institutionalized, in the interests of men.[15]

Regarding the biological and sociological factors of childbearing and -rearing as inextricable, Firestone postulates her primary demand for the liberation of women as follows:

> The freeing of women from the tyranny of their reproductive biology by every means available, and the diffusion of the childbearing and childrearing role to the society as a whole, men as well as women.[16]

In order to achieve this end, Firestone proposes the development of artificial reproduction. The question of artificial reproduction has always been controversial among feminists; many of them reject it as dangerous because it may be used against women by male scientists.[17] Firestone is aware of the dangers of artificial reproduction and considers the fears about it to be justified. Still she claims:

> But we are speculating about post-revolutionary systems, and for the purposes of our discussion we shall assume flexibility and good intentions in those working out the change.[18]

Artificial reproduction, according to Firestone, will destroy the family as basic social unit which upholds the patriarchal structure. Women and children will become economically - and consequently also socially and psychologically - independent from men (i.e. as husbands, fathers). They will be integrated fully into society and be able to follow a profession which fulfills their social and emotional needs and around which their lives will be organized. The elimination of the family will allow for various living arrangements, from single living to living in larger groups. Similarly, "humanity could finally revert to its natural

---

[15]Firestone, *The Dialectic of Sex*, p. 205.

[16]*ibid.*, p. 206.

[17]As an exemplification of this standpoint and a thorough critique of current reproductive technology and genetic manipulation, see Gena Corea, *The Mother Machine* (New York: Harper & Row, 1985).

[18]Firestone, *The Dialectic of Sex*, p. 206. The following outline of a post-revolutionary society is a summary of the chapter "The Ultimate Revolution," pp. 205-242.

polymorphous sexuality - all forms of sexuality would be allowed and indulged."[19] This would include homosexuality, polygamy, child sexuality and the elimination of the incest taboo.

All of these demands are fulfilled in *Woman on the Edge of Time* where there is absolutely no division of labor according to sex. Also, all forms of sexuality are allowed, even among children. Incest does not exist, due to artificial reproduction. A further parallel to Firestone's "cybernetic socialism"[20] in which technology would do away with all heavy toil, leaving people free to do creative work and to indulge in play, is found in *Woman on the Edge of Time* where machines do all the drudgery. Thus, people are free to develop their intellectual interests and follow their emotional needs. Their relationships are characterized by mutual respect and friendliness. If persons do not get along, as for instance Luciente and Bolivar, who are jealous of each other because of their lover Jackrabbit, they are requested to have a "worming". A worming is a public session in which the opponents lay open their criticism of each other and the community adds their own observations and comments. A neutral "judge" presides over the session. The opponents may be asked to try to communicate, or they are required not to talk to each other for a certain time, etc., depending on the outcome. Such measures are taken when somebody else suffers from a conflict (as does Jackrabbit, who is torn between his lovers, in the case above).

In this society based on democratic and egalitarian principles, sex-role division is supposedly rendered impossible. Still, Piercy also seems at times unable to escape the "traditional straitjackets" of gender-determined roles. So we find that women are still healers in the style of old wise women or witches (Diana, Erzulia); and the two sets of "coms" named in *Woman on the Edge of Time* consist each of two women and one man (Otter, Luxembourg - Bee; Otter, Luciente - Morningstar), thus leaving the impression that women still do more of the mothering. This is even strengthened by the fact that the head of the children's house, Magdalena, is a woman who is even "called" (i.e. mystically destined) to her profession.

In general, Piercy's underlying assumption seems to be that in peaceful surroundings and under a democratic system of equality on all levels people will be happy and friendly and violence will be a rare aberration for which healing will be offered - in case of repeated violence, however, the delinquent will be executed.

* * *

Gearhart's hill women are in a very different condition, compared to the societies in *The Left Hand of Darkness* and *Woman on the Edge of Time*. It is a relatively "young" society, trying to defend itself against its dystopian parent-society from which it split just one generation previously. With the creation of the Wanderground women's society Gearhart approaches the question of sex/gender roles from a completely different angle. Most notably, she is not at all concerned with a fusion or transcendence of gender-stereotypes on in the creation of a society where the sexes live together harmoniously. She is primarily concerned with what she perceives to be a crippling of women in a patriarchy. In her vision of a better world, Gearhart therefore creates an all-women sanctuary where women can fully develop their capacities in an unrestricted way. Sex/gender roles

---

[19]*ibid.*, p. 209.
[20]*ibid.*, p. 238.

are not thematized much in *The Wanderground*. Gearhart does not find it primarily necessary to rebel against the patriarchal construct of motherhood as the one role positively propagated for women and the major means to tie them down. Howard observes: "*The Wanderground* identifies male violence as the central fact of women's oppression, to the virtual exclusion of any other issue."[21]

Rape or the threat thereof is the major form of male violence. It is the most powerful weapon against women in the sexual realm, otherwise it finds expression in exploitation (taking something without permission). As an image for rape and exploitation, Gearhart chooses invasion as the worst crime. Troja, asking a guard in the out-post to mind-reach to her lover Rula-ji, who has gone to the desert on a mission, is worried because Rula-ji cannot be reached and asks the guard to "invade" her, i.e. to enter her mind without permission. This is called "man's crime." (*The Wanderground*, p. 70) Troja atones by singing the Wanderground version of the Demeter/Kore myth, which condemns the rape of Kore by the Lord of the Underworld: "Never may I enter where the way is not open, never may I take her if she does not choose to go."(*The Wanderground*, p. 75) LeGuin also hints at a connection between war and rape, the first possibly being "a purely masculine displacement-activity, a vast rape."(*The Left Hand of Darkness*, p. 67) Gearhart, in accord with her notion of biological determinism, includes heterosexuality (penetration) in the imagery of oppression, for instance when Clana muses on pornography:

> The guides had been careful time and again to tell them how it was not always like those pictures. They had said there was a difference between abusive sex between men and women and the kind which was a mutual expression of love. But Clana was still confused. How could you let someone enter your body that way and not be a victim? How could you ever want that to happen? (*The Wanderground*, p. 158)

The degrading status of the city women in *The Wanderground* seems to epitomize Gearhart's belief that the only roles men would grant women are those of ever-available sex-objects and of birth-machines: Men do not want women who work beside them, able to compete for a job, or women who reject them as sex-partners. So, when a city woman finds her death after trying to flee from a hill woman on rotation (whom she first considered to be a man, then, having discovered her sex, considers her a "dyke" - thus echoing Connie's initial confusion at Luciente in *Woman on the Edge of Time*), falling down several flights, a city man just remarks: "Well, she was too old to bear so it's no loss."(*The Wanderground*, p. 67)

This city woman, the only one ever described in detail, is an artificial antidote to the hill women:

> Ijeme looked at her unbelievingly. She was a thing out of history to the hill woman: a thickly painted face, lacquerstiffened hair, her body encased in a low-cut tight-fitting dress that terminated at mid-thigh; on her legs the thinnest of stockings, and the shoes - were they shoes? - Ijeme would not believe they fit the same part of anatomy that her own boots covered. How could she walk in these spindly things? . . .

---

[21]Howard, "Widening the Dialogue," p. 72. She mentions the influence of Mary Daly's *Gyn/Ecology* (1978), which emphasizes the "atrocities men have committed against women" (Howard), such as Chinese footbinding, Indian suttees etc.

This was the city edition, the man's edition, the only edition acceptable to men, streamlined to his expectations, her body guaranteed to be limited, dependent, and constantly available. (*The Wanderground*, p. 63)

"Misfit women" who do not conform to this standard are faced with male violence. We learn from the hill women's history in the remember rooms about a modern version of a witch hunt, "purges", etc. Women are hunted down and killed or sent to "behavior modification units" (drugs, brain manipulation - actually what happens to Connie and her co-inmates in the mental hospital, *The Wanderground*, pp. 152-153).[22]

This streamlining to only one (or two) functions is also deadly for women, which is metaphorically expressed in the fact that the city woman trips over her high-heeled shoes, which patriarchal ideas of female beauty require her to wear, and falls to her death. The hill women are very different in their looks and manner as they are not subject to patriarchal sex-roles. Seja, who meets the raped woman in armor at the beginning of *The Wanderground*, is a representative example: "Seja with her short curly hair, cotton shirt, soft trousers and sandals, her frank face and large hands open and out to the newcomer." (*The Wanderground*, p. 4) The readers learn only later what has happened to the strange woman in armor (i.e. that she has been raped, humiliated, and stuck into the armor by the rapists), but it is clear that she is running away from something and that she is afraid. Therefore, she feels threatened by Seja and her unfeminine looks, and threatens her in turn with her club and knife. In contrast to gender-stereotyped behavior, Seja is not afraid but self-confident in facing a potentially dangerous situation. She exposes her own vulnerability and peacefulness to the stranger in lying down before her without defence. Thereupon the stranger, who, as we have seen above, may be understood as a metaphor for women hurt and hardened in a patriarchy, allows Seja to strip her of her burdensome costume. Following the metaphor, this exemplifies the meaning of Gearhart's imagined sanctuary for women: the Wanderground is a place where women are free from patriarchal oppression, free as well from the need to defend themselves against it. Once they are stripped of all impediments imposed upon them, their true selves emerge.

Gearhart has elaborated on her ideas about women's true nature in her essays, most notably in "Womanpower: Energy Re-Sourcement." In *The Wanderground* she creates women in tune with what she calls their "intra-personal energy flow." The hill women are aware of their various levels of existence which determine them as a whole: their biology and physicality, their consciousness, their emotional life. This enables them to find their inner strength which is the source of their metaphysical skills.

Their balanced inner life and the awareness of their powers allows them to use their interpersonal energies in the way Gearhart imagines to be ideal. The women no longer feel any need to dominate, to exert power over one another. Instead, they realize their ties to nature, the earth, the cosmos as a whole - thus, they are able to communicate with plants, animals, and the elements themselves. As a consequence, the women develop a deep reverence for all life, including

---

[22]Cf. Gearhart's own real apprehensions in "Womanpower," p. 205: "I see, too, an ugly revival of orthodoxy within Christendom which could mean Witch hunts twentieth-century-style, complete with the use of satellite search and Kirlian photography . . . . when the backlash comes it will weirdo women who will be chased down first, arrested and separated from each other." Most recently, this fear has been fictionalized in Margaret Atwood's novel *The Handmaid's Tale* (1985).

mineral life. They become able to accept different forms of life and those laws of nature which seem cruel to us (e.g. they accept that the cougar is an animal of prey following its nature when it wants to feed on the dying pony in "Krueva and the Pony"). In the light of this attitude towards life it is only logical that they accept each other as they are. Their respect for each other and their equality with regard to their enormous powers renders all striving for dominance unnecessary, indeed it would be irrational. Moreover, their powers and the strong ties to their environment lead to a feeling of self-confidence and of being of value.

The Wanderground women's relationships are characterized by trust, cooperation, and loving care. Their telepathic skills allow very intimate forms of communication and interaction, as they not only consist in the mental transport of verbal messages, but also include the relay of feelings and moods in the form of colors, scents, and pictures, as well as in physical sensations such as "enfolding". Animals who live with the women (e.g. cats, dogs) are treated in the same way.

Violence and dislike are rare. In the latter case the women in question go through "sistersearch", a procedure very similar to Piercy's "worming". The only incidence of a violent attack of one woman upon another is really caused by men: Seja, after reliving the rape of the strange woman in her mind with physical sensation (a mental skill), is so upset that her perceptive faculties are clouded and she mistakes her lover Alaka for a rapist. Her anger is dealt with in a therapeutic way and she is not punished but treated with understanding and loving care.

It is important for the women to remain autonomous selves in spite of this network of love and care because any form of dependency (except the one of very young children upon elders) would be counter-productive to it. Love must be given and taken out of free will. Love relationships among the women are therefore neither exclusive nor possessive. Jealousy and possessiveness are considered obsolete, "old ways of trying to love" (*The Wanderground*, p. 4) which are cumbersome. Young Jacqua's thoughts and memories clarify the hill women's attitude:

> Two older sisters had spent too many days together without speaking their hearts to the rest. She knew the pattern, as young as she was. In fact, probably because she was so young. It was one of the first lessons of them all.
>
> Lightly in her memory she touched her long-ago warm soft days with Ursula, Ursula who had been her learntogether. She had not forgotten the feeling of needing for life itself Ursula's simple presence. They did not speak their warmness beyond each other to their sisters. They had become hidden with it. It began to eat away at their freestanding selves. Hence the saying: "There are no words more obscene than 'I can't live without you.' Count them the deepest affront to the person." Jacqua had not forgotten. In the end she had understood the importance of never feeling that way again. (*The Wanderground*, p. 3)

This passage closely resembles in content one in *Woman on the Edge of Time*, where the same attitude prevails. Luciente tells Connie:

> In truth, the most intense mating of my life was a woman named Diana - the fire that annealed me, . . . But it was a binding, you know, we obsessed. Not good for growing. We clipped each other. (*Woman on the Edge of Time*, p. 69)

Only LeGuin holds on to the notion of a pair of lovers dedicated to each other in the form of the Gethenian kemmering pair. Although she presents this model as the morally favored one, she nevertheless attempts to break up the (heterosexual) monogamous couple-model in offering kemmering groups or open promiscuity in public kemmering houses as socially accepted institutions. (One has to remember that Gethenian physiology includes an overwhelming sexual drive, therefore it is sanctioned and guilt-free.) So LeGuin's timid suggestion of a larger choice of life-styles is widened by Piercy and Gearhart alike to allow their autonomous utopian people to express their feelings for others sexually. Sexuality, truly liberated from patriarchal control (which establishes patrilinear lineage and guarantees immediate sexual gratification for men through the oppression, and even the exploitation, of women in prostitution, marital laws, or rape), becomes an unexploitative means of expressing affection, free from guilt and taboos.

* * *

The hill women, free from sex-role stereotypes, are mostly shown engaged in rituals or travelling through nature. It transpires that they grow their own food, build their shelters and so forth, but the women are never shown at work. Lefanu observes that "questions about food, clothing, building materials are left vague . . . . conception and childbirth too remain strangely out of focus."[23]

The question of conception in this all-female society is solved by a process of ovular merging and herbal treatment which is not explained in any detail at all. A child will have seven mothers, who contribute ova. One of them has an implantment and bears the child. In *The Wanderground* we only encounter one woman, Fora, who is going to be a mother. She is not, however, concerned with her role, but has a mystical experience at a place, the "deep cella", where she might have her implantment. Instead, Gearhart shows us a woman for whom children are a "carjery", i.e. she dislikes them:

> Fora saw something akin to disgust in Li's headshake. She pushed a short question around the look.
>
> Li responded. "It's children. They're not my favorite people. I need lots of distance from them still. I'm glad you're willing to take one on and I'll do my turns at the learnings but don't even hint that I be a sevensister much less a bearer . . ."
>
> In an instant Li's thoughts began to gather momentum. They proliferated and spun wider as is to dare the walls of the passageway to hold them back. A torrent of impatience and resentment began to pour out of Li. (*The Wanderground*, p. 44)

Li's resentment of children is not considered odd or unnatural. It is simply not a matter of importance at all. Gearhart here defies the patriarchal myth that all women at heart desire to be mothers. She claims instead that, free from patriarchal conditioning, some do not.

Children are fully integrated into the society; even at the age of three they participate fully in important rituals. (*The Wanderground*, p. 192) Gearhart says almost nothing in her novel about education and child-care, although she includes children in her stories. We may assume from the few references to children that they have considerable freedom in moving around and associating with whom they want, and that the whole community cares for them.

---

[23]Lefanu, *In the Chinks of the World Machine*, p. 67.

In this lack of emphasis on solving the question of childrearing, *The Wanderground* differs considerably from *The Left Hand of Darkness* and *Woman on the Edge of Time*. The latter novels struggle with the redefinition of one of the most influential roles for women and its social and political consequences. Gearhart, in refusing to define her notion of womanhood in contrast to the patriarchal one (as Piercy and LeGuin do) seems to presuppose that her readers are acquainted with Radical Feminist theory. In addressing her readership as a feminist one, she leaves out explanations based on such dialectics and moves on to the next step: the development of a notion of womanhood totally apart from patriarchal definitions as well as from reactions against these (cf. her use of the Amazon theme).

* * *

In this context, it may be interesting to look at the different ways in which the readers are asked to compare their own society to those portrayed in the novels. In *The Left Hand of Darkness*, this comparison is indirect. LeGuin describes Gethen in detail, whereas our own Western patriarchal culture is implied in Genly Ai. Genly is a socially conditioned patriarchal male who comes to question many of his biases and who develops an androgynous state of mind which in the end alienates him from his gender-determined shipmates.

In *Woman on the Edge of Time*, the two societies are directly compared: Connie's New York is fully portrayed and didactically compared to Mattapoisett. In the context of looking at sex-roles, the contrast is most obvious here particularly because Piercy deliberately draws parallels between people Connie knows or knew, and people in Mattapoisett. Thus, Connie's dead black lover Claud resembles Bee, her fellow inmate Sybil in the mental hospital could be Diana in the future Mattapoisett as both are witchlike, tall, and have auburn hair. The young homosexual inmate Skip shows similarities to Jackrabbit, and the dead old woman who is carelessly carted through the hospital could be Sappho, who is allowed to die with dignity in the future. Luciente's daughter Dawn reminds Connie painfully of her own daughter Angelina, and she herself could have been the Mexican judge Parra. Piercy underlines her intention of showing that in a favorable environment, everybody could grow into a healthy, strong person - particularly the people who are regarded as marginal, outcasts, or failures in our society - by drawing a parallel between Gildina in the dystopian future New York Connie once reaches accidentally, and Connie's niece Dolly. Gildina looks like a ridiculous "cartoon of femininity" after having repeatedly undergone cosmetic surgery. (*Woman on the Edge of Time*, p. 288) She uses drugs and is contracted as sex-object to a security agent. Dolly also uses drugs, dies her hair, controls her weight and works as a prostitute for pimps. In this way Piercy tries to get her message across, namely that one should work for a better future in which people could develop fully.

In *The Wanderground*, there are also two future societies, the Wanderground and the city. Both are to be compared to the present by the reader alone since there is no mediating visitor. The histroy of the Wanderground as it is given in the remember rooms is also a dystopian extrapolation of the present. It is a weakness with regard to the didactic intentions of *The Wanderground* that the ties between the utopian society and that of the reader are not more clearly established, although the provocative remarks about the "past" in *The Wanderground* will stimulate readers to compare their own society to the Wanderground.

The effort each of the authors puts into portraying the actual lives of the individuals in the alternative and/or utopian societies far exceeds that devoted to explaining the detailed functioning of these societies at all levels. All three authors are concerned most about how the individual feels about *living* there. Genly Ai's struggle to come to terms with Gethenian hermaphrodites and androgyny is appropriate to the concept of Gethen as a thought-experiment and may be representative of the reader's own reactions to it.

The parallels of present and future characters in *Woman on the Edge of Time* forcefully underline Piercy's passionate argument that an egalitarian society should be beneficial for each individual.

The Wanderground's lack of an obvious connection to the reader's world and the absence of the less pleasant aspects of a life in the wilderness prevents its conception of society in the end from being anything more than wishful thinking.

3.2 The Public Realm: Political Organization, Institutions, Social Structures

LeGuin, Piercy, and Gearhart have laid most emphasis on the portrayal of everyday life in their imaginative societies. On a larger scale, concerning the organization of work or of institutions, they are described far less explicitly, usually only in connection with people who happen to be in contact with institutions.

LeGuin, in her orientation towards anthropology, has been the least innovative and revolutionary in the invention of the political organization of the Gethenian nations. Karhide is a feudal monarchy and Orgoreyn a bureaucratic nation state. LeGuin has given more care to the delineation of Karhide because the characters spend more time there. The nation of Karhide is subdivided into "Domains" which are rather independent districts ruled by a Lord, whose powers are not specified. A Domain consists of several "Clan-Hearths" which are the original social unit of Gethen. From two hundred to eight hundred people live in a hearth. It is

> a structure founded less on economic convenience that on sexual necessity (there
> must be others in *kemmer* at the same time), . . . The hearth tends to be communal,
> independent, and somewhat introverted.[24]

It does not follow logically from this provision against sexual frustration that the "whole structure of the Karhidish Clan-Hearths and Domains is indubitably based on the institutions of monogamous marriage [i.e. vowing kemmering]." (*The Left Hand of Darkness*, p. 64) In "Is Gender Necessary?" LeGuin contradicts the above statement by the investigator Ong Tot Oppong:

> So the basic arrangement, I found, is that of the kemmerhouse, in every Gethenian
> community, which is open to anyone in kemmer, native or stranger, so that he can
> find a partner.[25]

---

[24]LeGuin, "Is Gender Necessary?" p. 164.
[25]*ibid.*, p. 167. According to the revised edition "[*read: so that they can find sexual partners*]" should be added to this quotation.

LeGuin's preference for and emphasis on pairbonding based on a moral commitment is probably a projection of her own opinion about morality, namely that the mature human being, male or female, is not satisfied by sexual gratification without psychic involvement.[26] In failing to elaborate on the connection between hearths and monogamy LeGuin could not account for what happens when two people from different hearths vow kemmernig. Who will follow whom into his clan?

The hearths and Domains have gathered into a seemingly unified nation which Genly Ai describes as

> a stew of uncoordinated principalities, towns, villages, "pseudofeudal tribal economic units," a sprawl and splatter of vigorous, competent, quarrelsome individualities over which a grid of authority was insecurely and lightly laid. (*The Left Hand of Darkness*, p. 69)

This "grid of authority" refers to the king - a ruler who usually possesses centralized power. The king of Karhide, however, does not possess such power, as is metaphorically expressed by the parade in the opening chapter where nobody marches in step. (*The Left Hand of Darkness*, pp. 2-3) At the end of the Gobrin Ice trek when Genly Ai and Estraven are taken in by Karhidish villagers who ask them who they are, the still outlawed and banned Estraven, who may not reveal his identity so as not to endanger his hosts, answers to the question whether he has been outlawed by king or clan: "The king shortens no man's shadow, though he may try," and Genly explains: "If Estraven's own clan had cast him out he would be a suspect character, but the king's strictures were unimportant." (*The Left Hand of Darkness*, p. 191)

The king thus has mainly representative functions - although it is not inherently logical that Karhide with her clan-structure should have one at all. LeGuin herself admits this flaw:

> I think I took the easy way in using such familiar governmental structures as a feudal monarchy and a modern-style bureaucracy for the two Gethenian countries that are the scene of the novel. I doubt that Gethenian governments, rising out of the cellular "hearth," would resemble any of our own so closely.[27]

The underlying anarchy of Karhidish structure, the loose collection of Domains, is endangered by the efforts of Estraven's enemy Tibe to increase the centralized power in order to turn Karhide into a centrally controlled nation state. LeGuin depicted a moment at which the balance between the (anarchic) female and the male principles, having slightly tipped towards the feminine, is now moving towards the opposite pole.[28] There is a resemblance between Karhide, her "feminine" Domains and "masculine" king, and matriarchal societies in which the clan mothers hold the real power and are the main decision-makers,

---

[26]*ibid.*, p. 166. LeGuin here explains her beliefs more fully. She draws on anthropology and on analogies to animal life in order to underline her point of view that human beings do not truly desire genuine license. Monogamy, however, is actually rare: "Comparatively few societies limit their members to one spouse apiece; in most societies it is considered desirable to have more than one." Vivelo, *Cultural Anthropology Handbook*, p. 170.

[27]LeGuin, "Is Gender Necessary?" p. 167.

[28]*ibid.*, p. 165.

whereas the men represent the clan in the public life.[29] If the latter misuse their power they endanger the harmony of the matriarchal society.

About Orgoreyn, the other important nation on Gethen, little is said. She is an efficient bureaucracy, there are elections, factions (parties), a parliament, a police, a secret service, but we are not told how they are constituted and how they function. The division into social classes is more strictly hierarchic than that in Karhide. Furthermore, in contrast to Karhide, it does have economic consequences. The family-clan does not exist here any longer. Orgoreyn resembles a Western industrialized nation and is far less favorably described than Karhide.

* * *

Another important area of public life is that of science. We learn nothing about the educational systems on Gethen but the Gethenians have developed technology on a high standard. They do not, however, exploit the natural resources of their planet. Genly Ai connects this lack of a drive towards progress expressed in their living always in the Year One, to the dictates of Gethen's climate:

> Along in those four millenia the electric engine was developed, radios and power looms and power vehicles and farm machinery and all the rest began to be used, and a Machine Age got going, gradually, without any industrial revolution, without any revolution at all. Winter hasn't achieved in thirty centuries what Terra once achieved in thirty decades. Neither has Winter ever paid the price that Terra paid.
>
> Winter is an inimical world, its punishment for doing things wrong is sure and prompt: death from cold or death from hunger. No margin, no reprieve. A man can trust his luck, but a society can't; and cultural change, like random mutation, may make things chancier. So they have gone very slowly. At any one point in their history a hasty observer would say that all technological progress and diffusion had ceased. Yet it never has. Compare the torrent and the glacier. Both get where they are going.
> (*The Left Hand of Darkness*, pp. 68-69)

Although the glacial climate of Gethen stands in the way of indentifying it with Earth, the criticism of "Terran" obsession with speedy progress in science and technology is obviously implied. The present problems of pollution and exploitation of natural resources make things chancy for our world, too.

* * *

In Luciente's Mattapoisett people are also very careful with regard to science and ecology. In answer to Connie's exclamation "You must still have mosquitos!" Luciente explains:

> They're part of the food chain. We bred out the irritant . . .. About weather, when it gets disastrous, sometimes we adjust a little. But every region must agree. When a region is plagued by drought, grasp, wc usually prefer to deliver food than to approve a weather shift. Because of the danger. We're cautious about gross experiments. 'In

---

[29]The Hopi are one example. See LeBow, "Rethinking Matriliny Among the Hopi." Cf. also Heide Göttner-Abendroth, "Melpomene - Tragödie des Eros," *Für die Musen* (Frankfurt a.M.: Zweitausendeins, 1988) pp. 92-102.

bio-systems, all factors are not knowable.' First rule when we study living beings in relation. (*Woman on the Edge of Time*, p. 97)

In contrast to this attitude, Bee characterizes present-day scientists in the following way:

> Your scientists were so . . . childish? Carefully brought up through a course of study entered on early never to ask consequences, never to consider a broad range of effects, never to ask on whose behalf . . . (*Woman on the Edge of Time*, p. 196)

Luciente, in an effort to explain to Connie that there is not really a difference between effects and side effects, describes the above mentioned broad range thus:

> A factory may also produce pollution - which takes away drinking water downstream. Dead fish we can't eat. Diseases or gene defects. These too are products of that factory. A factory uses up water, power, space. It uses up time, the lives of those who work in it. If the work is boring and alienating, it produces bored, angry people -. (*Woman on the Edge of Time*, p. 276)

Thus, all dull, heavy and/or dangerous work (e.g. mining) has been automatized, although due regard is paid to the fact that energy sources are limited (sun, wind, decomposing wastes, waves, rivers, alcohol from wood, wood gas - cf. *Woman on the Edge of Time*, p. 129).

The decisions about developments and directions in science are brought about by the whole community. Thus, scientific research is subject to the democratic system and not, as in present-day industrialism, to the powerful and wealthy (cf. *Woman on the Edge of Time*, p. 278). Researchers and scientists check each others' work for validity - who is checked by whom is decided by lot. The community, however, decides on the nature and purpose of research products in the first place because everybody is affected. Connie is surprised by the idea that she could decide on scientific matters in Mattapoisett: "You mean by people like me? How could I decide if they should build an atom bomb or something?" (*Woman on the Edge of Time*, p. 277) Luciente retorts:

> Of course you could decide. It affects you - how not? A rep from the base [i.e. research project] talks. On the local level for a small proj. But if it is a major proj. - such as research on prolonging life would be - then everybody decides. What it would cost to begin. What it would use up in the way of resources and labor. All that would be set out. (*Woman on the Edge of Time*, p. 277)

In contrast to this, present-day scientists do not even inform the people whom they use in their research projects as "guinea pigs". (*Woman on the Edge of Time*, p. 144) Today's science does not respect living beings:

> [Connie] remembered something she had heard Dr. Redding say to Superintendent Hodges: that they had used up five thousand monkeys before they began doing these operations on patients. Used up. She had heard him say he had wanted to work with prisoners - he thought the results would be more impressive - but there had been such an uproar about three little psychosurgical procedures at Vacaville in California that his team decided to work with mental patients. "After all," he had said, smiling his best ironic smile, "they made a court case and a bleeding heart

publicity brouhaha about three procedures, while San Francisco Children's Hospital does hundreds with sound and thermal probes - mostly on neurotic women and intractable children - and no one says boo." (*Woman on the Edge of Time*, pp. 220-221)

This arrogance and misused power stands in sharp contrast to the democratic system of Mattapoisett. All people are considered capable of decision-making as all are equally concerned. Therefore there are no specialized politicians who are elected to posts, who may be reelected and who thus gain power. Instead, serving the society on the decision-making level is a task like any other which should be done by everybody at least once in their lives. In order to ensure this equality and to prevent a person from gaining power at an important post, the representatives are not elected but chosen by lot. They serve for a year: three months with their predecessor, six months on their own, and three months with their successor. Two special positions are exceptions to this rule: the Earth Advocate and the Animal Advocate, who speak for the rights of the total environment and for all animals respectively. They are called to their posts by dream: if several persons dream they are the new Advocates, the choice falls by lot. (*Woman on the Edge of Time*, p. 151) The representatives do not hold speeches - in fact, there is a five-minute limit on speeches - but argue quietly and freely among themselves. (*Woman on the Edge of Time*, p. 150) Luciente describes the procedure for decisions about ecology and environmental affairs:

> We arrive with the needs of each village and try to divide scarce resources justly. Often we must visit the spot. Next level is regional planning. Reps chosen by lot from township level go to the regional to discuss gross decisions. The needs go up and the possibilities come down. If people are chilled by a decision, they go and argue. Or they barter directly with places needing the same resources, and compromise. (*Woman on the Edge of Time*, p. 152)

This method of taking decisions is strenuous - particularly because there is no final authority and no majority decision. Connie is incredulous because she is used to final authorities, to a centralized power. She is told by Luciente and another acquaintance:

> "We argue till we close to agree. We just continue. Oh, it's disgusting sometimes. It bottoms you."
> "After a big political fight, we guest each other," the man said. "The winners have to feed the losers and give presents." (*Woman on the Edge of Time*, pp. 153-154)

Decisions of far-reaching consequences are taken differently, by vote. Luciente explains:

> Grasp, political decisions - like whether to raise or lower population - go a different route. We talk locally and then choose a rep to speak our posit on area hookup. Then we all sit in holi simulcast and the rep from each group speaks their village posit. Then we go back into local meeting to fuse our final word. Then the reps argue once more before everybody. Then we vote. (*Woman on the Edge of Time*, p. 154)

Piercy has given great care to the outline of this process, but she did not elaborate on its possible range: How large is the area for which a decision is made? Is it nationwide, or even worldwide? The larger the area, the more cumbersome and difficult it will be to arrive at a decision.

Piercy, however, does not neglect to emphasize that equality in rights and powers also requires the individuals of her utopian society to be responsible. They have to realize the need for their active participation. So, when Connie wryly remarks: "You must spend an awful lot of time in meetings," Luciente replies: "How can people control their lives without spending a lot of time in meetings?" (*Woman on the Edge of Time*, p. 154) A refusal or neglection to take one's responsibilities seriously is interpreted as a lack of interest in the community. Connie is told in answer to her question what happens if people do not want to attend meetings:

> Who could force you? People would ask you why you no longer care. Friends might suggest you take a retreat or talk to a healer. If your mems felt you'd cut them off, they might ask you to leave. (*Woman on the Edge of Time*, p. 154)

The same applies to work ethic. The coordination of work in a "base" (i.e. a work unit) is done by lot in order to ensure that dull and exciting tasks are distributed equally and justly. All members are regarded as equally capable. Although a current saying is Mattapoisett: "Person must not do what person cannot do," (*Woman on the Edge of Time*, p. 101, *et passim*) a person who does not work at all will be socially ostracized. Connie and Luciente discuss this:

> "Ever hear of being lazy? Suppose I just don't want to get up in the morning."
> "Then I must do your work on top of my own if I'm in your base. Or in your family, I must do your defense or your childcare. I'll come to mind that. Who wants to be resented? Such people are asked to leave and they may wander from village to village sourer and more self-pitying as they go. We sadden at it." (*Woman on the Edge of Time*, p. 101)

Such "drifters" are the only suspicious people in the future of Mattapoisett.

* * *

Otherwise, all people in the community are included in social life, even children and people of old age. Children live in a children's house but they are fully integrated into society because they participate in public life and work. Only young children up to five years play with toys in order to learn coordination and dexterity. Older children join the adults at work: on the fields, in the laboratories, in the clinics and so forth. They don't go to school but learn by practice. Also, they come to understand the necessity for everyone to participate and to take responsibility. Magdalena, the head of the house of children, tells Connie: "When children aren't kept out of the real work, they don't have the same need for imitation things." (*Woman on the Edge of Time*, p. 137) Thus, everybody is a teacher and instructs the children. Old people in particular are considered fit for this task. (*Woman on the Edge of Time*, p. 132)

The children learn voluntarily and may study what they feel they are interested in. In order to do so, they are able to use highly complex technology as well as a library complete with computers and "holigraphs". Furthermore, they are also taught how to control body reactions to feelings, a discipline called "inknowing". Magdalena explains to Connie: "In your day some of it was called yoga, some meditating, some biofeedback, some had no name at all." (*Woman on the Edge of Time*, p. 140) Luciente adds:

> [W]e want to prevent overreacting - heart attacks, indigestion, panic. We want to get used to knowing exactly what we feel, so we don't shove on other people what's coming from inside. (*Woman on the Edge of Time*, p. 140)

Magdalena sums up the all-encompassing program for children's education: "We educate the senses, the imagination, the social being, the muscles, the nervous system, the intuition, the sense of beauty - as well as memory and intellect." (*Woman on the Edge of Time*, p. 140) Thus, children grow up being almost full members of the society, and their voluntary work-input relieves the community. Since the children have three mothers and the community to take care of them, they grow up feeling valued and loved. Luciente explains the difference between present-day notions of child-rearing and the utopian ones in Mattapoisett:

> It's not the one-to-one bind you had with your daughter, from what you say. We've more space, more people to love us. We grow up closest to our mothers, but we swim close to all our mems - or some, at least! . . . It's hard for me to inknow what it would feel like to love only *one* and have only *one* soul to love me. (*Woman on the Edge of Time*, p. 133)

As long as the children have not reached puberty and undergone "naming", the *rite de passage* for adulthood, which is modelled on Amerindian ones[30], they are taken care of in the house of children but they are already part of a "family". This is a social unit which is not based on genetic or biological bonds because these no longer exist. Instead, the family is formed by individuals ("mems") who like each other and who have formed emotional ties. Luciente and some others distinguish their lovers and special friends as "core", a smaller unit than the family. Apart from the fact that families share a table in the communal dining hall, apparently no exclusive activities for "mems" exist. A family is a loose network of friends.

Several families make up a village, which consists of about six hundred people. Apart from communal dining halls and work places, every adult lives in separate huts or rooms.

In order to maintain cultural diversity, each village is adapted to a culture, such as American Indian (Wamponaug in Luciente's case), Harlem-Black, European Jewish, Portuguese and so forth. Bee tells Connie:

> At grandcil - grand council - decisions were made forty years back to breed a high proportion of darker-skinned people and to mix the genes well through the population. At the same time, we decided to hold on to separate cultural identities. But we broke the bond between genes and culture, broke it forever. We want there to be no chance of racism again. But we don't want the melting pot where everybody ends up with thin gruel. We want diversity, for strangeness breeds richness. (*Woman on the Edge of Time*, p. 103-104)

Piercy has been thorough in her attempt to include most aspects necessary to the description of a functioning utopia. She has given considerable care to those

---

[30]See Vivelo, *Cultural Anthropology Handbook*, p. 189, for the description of such a rite among North American Plains Indians.

aspects which present problems in Piercy's own culture, i.e. racism, misuse of power in science, government and so forth.

* * *

Due to her different intentions, Gearhart has addressed the area of politics, institutions, and social structure in *The Wanderground* in a far less detailed way. The hill women of the Wanderground area - a map is given as frontispiece - live in four basic communities: in two villages, the Eastern and Western Ensconcements; in the Kochlias, a mountain with a labyrinth of caves and tunnels, and in the various Outposts at the Wanderground border. Several hundred women live in the Wanderground. The guards at the Outposts do not stay there permanently but are relieved by other women regularly. The Kochlias is the center of learning and education, whereas the inhabitants of the ensconcements are responsible for agriculture.

As in Piercy's Mattapoisett, every woman inhabits her own living quarters, her "nest". It is open to her choice how she builds it: in a tree, or as a hut, or a deserted house. Provisions are communally owned and centrally stored in a barn.

* * *

Three women ("Three-Fold") in each of the four communities form the "Long Dozen":

> The Long Dozen - long because there was always another created - came together across the hills every evening of the term. They brought to each other for sharing or decision all the woman-matters, from threats of external danger to work rotations or the discovery of a covey of quail at a meadow's edge. (*The Wanderground*, p. 122)

In accord with her emphasis on the immediate experience of life in her imaginative society, Gearhart has included the "gathering chant" for the purely telepathic meeting of the Long Dozen but does not, however, care to explain how the Long Dozen is chosen, how long each woman serves, and what exactly its functions are. Basically it seems to be a news relay. Apart from the fact that work and tasks rotate, the reader is never told how this system of rotation functions.

Most of the decision-making process is also left in the dark. Gearhart does not explicitly say that the Long Dozen has any power to decide on anything - if there are matters on which it takes decisions, the reader is not told which these are. For questions and decisions which concern more women, a whole community, or the whole Wanderground, the women come together in a "gatherstretch", a telepathic linking of those women who consider the matter at issue to be important.

One story/chapter, "The Gatherstretch" (*The Wanderground*, pp. 118-132), tells about this procedure. The issue to be discussed is a difficult one: Should the women meet with the Gentles, cooperate with them? After all the women have joined mentally, one of the Long Dozen presents the matter in detail and also includes the thoughts and discussions of the Long Dozen on that matter so far. Other women then contribute their knowledge. The effect of the "Revolt of the Earth", namely that men cannot rape or kill outside the city, that animals refuse to be their beasts of burden, and that exploitative technology does not function, seems to be waning. Women who have been on rotation in the city and women who found killed animals outside of the city confirm the observations. The

Gentles obviously have made similar ones and seem to have a plan to share with the women. Some of the women, however, strictly refuse to deal with any men at all. As the dissent is very serious, the women remind themselves of their anarchism by a ritual called "The Regard of Tui."[31] It consists of two "acknowledgements" in the form of questions to be answered. The first question is: "Can we, on both sides of the matter, yield?" (*The Wanderground*, p. 129) The second question is asked by Li:

> I am called to remind us that at any moment we can cease to be one body. No woman has to follow the will of any other. Always we must know that we can separate, even splinter or disperse one-by-one, for a little while or forever. We rest our unity on that possibility. (*The Wanderground*, p. 129)

The agreement to this acknowledgement means that the basic anarchic requirement is fulfilled: no power of anyone over somebody else. This excludes majority decisions. Instead, the group will split if an unanimous agreement cannot be reached. In the gatherstretch the women argue for a very long time about the pros and cons of cooperation with the Gentles. Just as Piercy has Luciente state that such a procedure is tiring and unnerving, Gearhart shows the strain of the women' effort: "The anger was hot; accusations and counter-accusations raged. A bone-deep weariness spread among the women. It seemed that no clear wish could be reached." (*The Wanderground*, p. 130) In the case given in *The Wanderground*, the women ultimately find a solution that is accepted as a "clear wish": three women will meet with the Gentles, but they may speak only for themselves, not for the whole community of the Wanderground. The possibility of fission from the society of the Wanderground women in case of insurmountable disagreements - such fissions have actually occured in its history - render this aspect of *The Wanderground* more realistic than its counterpart in *Woman on the Edge of Time*. Piercy seems to beg the question that disagreements may not be settled by endless discussions. In her utopian design, people may leave a place if they no longer care to live there, but this does not seem to suffice as a solution in a hypothetical case where an unanimous decision cannot be reached.

* * *

As far as the other aspects of public life which are examined in this section are concerned, namely education and science, *The Wanderground* remains rather vague. We are never told what the tasks of the seven mothers are. Children have other children as "learntogethers", but Gearhart never says what they learn, and from whom. When the girls are about six to seven years old they are taken to the Kochlias in order to learn. They learn the Wanderground history in the remember rooms, via telepathic transfer (i.e. in a dreamlike way, they "relive" the adventures of former hill women without experiencing their physical pain). The girls also learn certain skills such as windriding (levitation, "flying"), toting (telekinesis), healing, and many more. Telepathic abilities seem to be innate and are developed in the same way as we learn speech.

* * *

---

[31]*Tui* is one of the sixty-four signs of the *I Ching*, the old Chinese "Book of Transformations." I shall further elaborate on its use in *The Wanderground* in the following section on religion and mysticism.

Science, in our sense of the word, does not exist in the Wanderground. The hill women regard our present-day science as necessary in order to build machines or to develop technology, i.e. it is seen as an inadequate substitute for fully developed innate mental capacities.[32] Thus, the Kochlias relic-keeper Rhynna tells the girl-child Clana: "We can do anything the old machines could do. And with a good deal less effort." (*The Wanderground*, p. 145) To Clana's question: "Then why don't we do them, Rhynna?" the latter answers in accord with Gearhart's own opinion about science and technology as it has been developed by men:

> That's the mistake the men made, sisterlove, and made over and over again. Just because it was possible they thought it had to be done. They came near to destroying the earth - and may yet - with that notion. Most of us like to think that even long ago women could have built what's been called "western civilization"; we know how to do all of it but we rejected most such ideas as unnecessary or destructive. (*The Wanderground*, p. 145)

It is interesting to note that Gearhart, although, like Piercy, she implicitly criticizes present-day scientists for their lack of responsibility on a larger scale, she does this from a different point of view. Whereas Piercy relegates the defects of contemporary science to economics (capitalism) and concomitant greed, exploitation, and selfishness, Gearhart locates the faults in the male psyche, part of which seems to be a hypertrophic urge towards extremes: to push towards limits because it is possible, regardless of the consequences. In Gearhart's opinion the female psyche is exempt from such anomalies.

In contrasting these two analyses one may well criticize Gearhart's notions as being too simple. Piercy's focus on the importance of economic interests and power with regard to science implies that since women never had any consequential access to power and economic means, they could not exert any influence on science. Therefore, women are less guilty that men, as Luciente says: "Yet I can't see male and female as equally to blame, for one had power and the other was property." (*Woman on the Edge of Time*, p. 211)

In Gearhart's approach, the fact that women neither had access to power nor to science is simply ignored. Instead, Gearhart seems to suggest that women *chose* not to participate in the development of (male) science, probably because of their "better" nature. According to Piercy's analysis, this choice would render them guilty of present-day defects, indeed. Piercy's analysis with regard to the connection between sexism and economy is based on much firmer ground than Gearhart's assumption of a difference between male and female natures which is ultimately a matter of personal belief.

LeGuin's point of view seems to be close to Gearhart's in that she connects masculinity with a linear drive towards progress, which is balanced by a feminine tendency towards cyclic procedure. The balance is tipped towards the masculine in our world, therefore science has run rampant. It is important to remember, however, that LeGuin perceives human beings as being psychologically androgynous, thus possessing both masculine and feminine qualities; the balance

---

[32] I have said in the previous discussion of *The Wanderground* (2.3) that parapsychology and esoterics are used as background sciences. Within the novel, however, parapsychological phenomena are devoid of a "scientific" aspect, i.e. they are not subject to our own notions of what is scientific or empirical. They belong to the system of mysticism within *The Wanderground*.

between these must be restored to each individual. Therefore, she does not postulate different natures of the sexes.

* * *

On the whole, Piercy has been most thorough in the treatment of the public aspects of her utopian conception of a future society. Because of its limited scope, a work of fiction cannot describe a societal system as fully as a tract such as Plato's *Republic*.

The inconsistencies of *The Left Hand of Darkness* in this respect are the result of LeGuin's walking a thin rope between the intention to mirror our own world as it is - which would account for the use of familiar governmental structures which are unlikely to be indigenous of hermaphroditic/androgynous societies - and the intention to point to an apparently unrecognized positive quality in humanity, namely its psychological androgyny, which in itself points towards a utopian future. LeGuin's model differs strongly from that of *Woman on the Edge of Time* and *The Wanderground* because it does not relegate all social ills to the issue of sexual oppression.

Gearhart has given very little details of the organization of her concept of a better society. The instances of decision-making in *The Wanderground* just barely suffice to underline the anarchic organization of society. This lack of explaining societal structure undermines the utopian aspect of *The Wanderground*, makes it impossible to outline its "historical" development, and is also responsible for part of the novel's elusiveness.

3.3 Religion and Mysticism

A full conception of an alternative society has to include aspects of human nature and community which deal with the questions about the sense of life, the meaning of death, the basis of ethics and morals. These are the realms of philosophy, religion, and mysticism.

Of the novels examined in this thesis, only *The Left Hand of Darkness* features institutionalized religions. In *Woman on the Edge of Time* and *The Wanderground* explicit religions and/or philosophies do not exist. The people of those utopian societies, however, have an attitude towards nature that carries religious overtones.

None of the novels endorses Christianity, the dominant religion of the U.S.A. Feminists consider it to be misogynist. The concept of an omnipotent male deity and the concomitant ideology of female inferiority and of a hierarchy with centralized power, as in institutionalized churches, certainly have no appeal to feminism and its basically anarchic (or at least democratic) orientation and its ideology of sexual equality. As Luciente says in *Woman on the Edge of Time*, "god is a patriarchal concept." (*Woman on the Edge of Time*, p. 104)

* * *

The Left Hand of Darkness features two distinct religions: the Handdara religion and the Yomesh cult. The Handdara religion is by far the older of the two, dating back about thirteen thousand years. As the Yomesh cult, which is a proselyte of the Handdara, is only two thousand years old, the Handdara has been shaping Gethenian thinking and society for an immensely long period.

After his unsuccessful audience with the king, Genly Ai has time to spend in Karhide and decides to increase his knowledge of the Handdara. He visits a "Fastness", which is something akin to a monastery. Upon his arrival at Otherhord Fastness, Genly summarizes his knowledge of the Handdara, which he has so far acquired through hearsay only:

> The Handdara is a religion whithout institution, without priests, without hierarchy, without vows, without creeds; I am still unable to say whether is has a God or not. It is elusive. It is always somewhere else. Its only fixed manifestation is in the Fastnesses, retreats to which people may retire and spend the night or a lifetime. (*The Left Hand of Darkness*, p. 38)

This anarchic structure is in accord with LeGuin's own attraction towards anarchy, which is, for her, the most idealistic and most interesting of all political theories.[33] The Handdara permeates Karhide in its own special, unobtrusive way: "Under that nation's politics and parades and passions runs an old darkness, passive, anarchic, silent, the fecund darkness of the Handdara." (*The Left Hand of Darkness*, p. 42) The Handdara "darkness" consists of two basic principles: "ignorance", and inactivity or non-interference. (*The Left Hand of Darkness*, p. 41) These are also the characteristics of the Tao philosophy as it is outlined by the Chinese philosopher Lao-tzu in his *Tao te Ching*.

The principle of inactivity and non-interference is based on the idea that every act, every move, will provoke a counter-movement. Richard Wilhelm sums up this aspect of the *Tao te Ching* in the following way:

> When everybody in the world recognizes the good as good, that which is not good is already implied . . . In every instance a position necessarily calls forth its negation . . . . . Every transgression of an individual will call forth a balancing reaction on the part of the disturbed order of the world.[34]

In order to avoid this involuntary but inevitable strengthening of the opposite position by one's own action, the sage refrains from taking actions and leaves the development of things to the workings of the Tao, the basic cosmic force which cannot be explained, the origin of all things. Lao-tzu describes the workings of the Tao in paragraph 21 of the *Tao te Ching*:

> The contents of LIFE follows the WAY [Tao]. The WAY brings about things, chaotic, dark. Chaotic, dark are the images in it. Dark, chaotic, are the things in it. Unfathomably dark is essence in it. This essence in wholly true. Authenticity is in it.[35]

The image of the seed is an appropriate one to describe the laws of Tao, which are actually far from being "chaotic":

---

[33] See Ursula K. LeGuin, Preface to "The Day Before the Revolution," in *The Wind's Twelve Quarters: Short Stories by Ursula K. LeGuin* (New York: Harper & Row, 1975) p. 232. She also states here that she considers anarchism to be prefigured in early Taoist thought.

[34] Richard Wilhelm, Introd. *Tao te king*, by Laotse (Köln: Diederichs, Gelbe Reihe, 1978), pp. 30-31. Author's translation.

[35] Laotse, *Tao te king*, trans. Richard Wilhelm (Köln: Diederichs, Gelbe Reihe, 1978) p. 61. Author's translation. English - as well as German - translations of the *Tao te Ching* (*Tao te king*) are numerous and differ widely. My arguments are based on this edition/translation, therefore I chose to translate from it into English rather than choosing among various alternatives in English.

Thus it is necessary to recognize in all things their essence. . . . All these laws are concerned not with a necessity imposed from without but an immanent organic vitality unfolds itself freely according to the law of entelechy.[36]

LeGuin herself explains:

The Taoist world is orderly, not chaotic, but its order is not imposed by man or by a personal or humane deity. The true laws - ethical and aesthetic, as surely as scientific - are not imposed from above by any authority but exist in things and are to be found - discovered.[37]

Obviously there exist similarities between the Tao and the "female principle" as LeGuin perceives it (see 2.3). The sage will attempt not to obstruct the workings of the Tao by his own interfering actions, so that it can unfold its own perfect order:

Therefore the emphasis on non-activity. This non-activity is not idleness, but absolute receptivity for that which unfolds itself from its metaphysical root in every individual. This is the meaning of the various passages which denote LIFE as something feminine, purely receptive. This LIFE is good insofar as it shows the appropriate action in every moment and in every situation.[38]

This receptivity is practiced by the Handdarata discipline of "Presence", a special kind of meditation:

[The Handdarata discipline of Presence] is a kind of trance - the Handdarata, given to negatives, call it an untrance - involving self-loss (self-augmentation?) through extreme sensual receptiveness and awareness. Though the technique is the exact opposite of most techniques of mysticism it probably is a mystical discipline, tending towards the experience of Immanence. (*The Left Hand of Darkness*, p. 40)

This concept of immanence is related to the Taoist concept of the reduction of knowledge. Lao-tzu says in paragraph 48 of the *Tao te Ching*:

He who exercises the art of learning, multiplies daily. He who exercises the WAY, diminishes daily. He diminishes and diminishes until he arrives at non-activity. Non-activity will leave nothing undone.[39]

Faxe expresses a similar doctrine: "The unknown . . . is what life is based on. Ignorance is the ground of thought. Unproof is the ground of action." (*The Left Hand of Darkness*, p. 49) The reduction of knowledge is intrinsic to Taoist epistemology. The seeds in the Tao and their ensuing reality can be named in our world with the help of language. As long as the words of the language are related to the being of the designated object (the signifier-signified relation), the creation of an order is possible. Wilhelm delineates the further process of

---

[36]Richard Wilhelm, "Kommentar - Die Lehren des Laotse," in Laotse, *Tao te king*, p. 132. Author's translation.

[37]Ursula K. LeGuin, "Dreams Must Explain Themselves," in *The Language of the Night*, p. 49. First published in *Algol*, 21 (1973).

[38]Wilhelm, Introd. *Tao te king*, p. 30. Author's translation.

[39]Laotse, *Tao te king*, p. 91. Author's translation.

digression from the Tao through the misunderstanding and misuse of knowledge and its instrument, language:

> Knowledge is won with the help of comparison and definition, it is therefore necessarily bound to the world of appearances, which is split up into polar opposites.
> This, however, has further consequences. The human being has in concepts tools of the knowledge of reality, he can use these concepts independently. He can generate concepts which do not have an original equivalent (Urbild) in his reality. . . . According to Lao-tzu, this is the original fall. . . . The more precise reason will work, the more precise will knowledge be, and the farther humanity will be led from the WAY. Therefore it is Lao-tzu's opinion that one should not participate in culture and knowledge, but one should instead practice simple integration into the context of nature. In the face of an exaggerated development of the rational, one should return to a nameless unity, to that state which allows the harmless unfolding of the Tao, empty of the desire to describe it with the help of names, because the connection between the great mother and her child, man, has been restored.[40]

This is the attitude which kept Gethen in general and Karhide in particular from developing a hypertrophic, progress-oriented technology and which influenced her concept of science. The Karhiders have invented only such machines and devices which are necessary to keep them alive.

* * *

The holistic concept of the cosmos as outlined in Lao-tzu's Tao is connected to the concept of androgyny because the balance of the Tao is based on the equilibrium of polarities, which are continuously created by it.

> The Book of Transformations [*I Ching*, another major text of the Tao philosophy] contains the view that the whole world of appearances is based on the polar oppositions of forces; the creative and the receptive, One and Two, light and shadow, positive and negative, masculine and feminine, all these are appearances and manifestations of the polar forces which bring about all change and transformation. These forces are not to be taken as resting primal forces. The point of view of the Book of Transformations is far from any cosmic dualism. Instead, these forces are in perpetual transformation themselves. One splits up and becomes Two, Two unite to become One.[41]

The polarities listed here are identical with those found by Baumann in connection with androgyny (cf. 2.1). LeGuin's concept of psychological androgyny can be traced to paragraph 28 of the *Tao te Ching*:

> He who knows his manhood and retains his womanhood, he is the crevice of the world. When he is the crevice of the world, he will never be deserted from eternal LIFE, and he will be like a child again.[42]

The use of Taoist principles in *The Left Hand of Darkness* contributes to the ultimate thematic unity of the novel.

---

[40]Wilhelm, "Kommentar," pp. 143-145. Author's translation.
[41]*ibid.*, p. 130. Author's translation.
[42]Laotse, *Tao te king*, p. 68. Author's translation.

The Handdarata discipline of "Foretelling" at first does not seem to fit into the Taoist doctrine. The mystical practice of "Foretelling" provides a method of predicting the future accurately. It is described in the fifth chapter ("The Domestication of Hunch") where Genly Ai asks the foretellers whether Gethen will be a member of the Ekumen within five years; he receives a positive answer. Faxe, the Weaver (i.e a "director" of foretellings), directs the tensions among the participants of the ritual: five celibate Handdarata who are adepts of "Presence", one celibate Handdarata entering kemmer, one "Pervert" (i.e. a Gethenian individual in permanent kemmer, thus being permanently male or female), and two "Zanies" (schizophrenics). The interwoven tensions of frustrated sexuality (celibate kemmerer - Pervert), "presencing"- and the distorted sense of time of the Zanies enable the Weaver to reach a short moment of *"seeing everything at once*: seeing whole." (*The Left Hand of Darkness*, p. 143) Past, present, and future are all seen simultaneously. Genly, however, learns from Faxe that the Handdarata perfected Foretelling only in order "[t]o exhibit the perfect uselessness of knowing the answer to the wrong question." (*The Left Hand of Darkness*, p. 49) The Handdarata come to the Fastness in order to learn which questions not to ask. Estraven, in his Mishnory exile, reasons: "To learn which questions are unanswerable, and *not to answer them*: this skill is most needful in times of stress and darkness." (*The Left Hand of Darkness*, p. 107) The deeper meaning of this insight is illustrated by the hearth tale about Lord Berosty, whose question "On what day shall I die?" was answered "You will die on Odstreth (the nineteenth day of any month)." (*The Left Hand of Darkness*, p. 30) The answer eventually causes his madness, the death of his kemmering, and ultimately his own suicide.

* * *

Meshe, who originally was a Handdara Weaver, founded the Yomesh cult after having been forced to answer an "unanswerable" question (i.e. a question that is rejected by the Weaver) asked by the Lord of Shorth: "What is the meaning of life?" (*The Left Hand of Darkness*, p. 42) This origin of the cult is marked by force and an unauthorized question and its anwer. The result was disastrous:

> The Foretellers stayed in the darkness for six days and nights. At the end, all the
> Celibates were catatonic, the Zanies were dead, the Pervert clubbed the Lord of
> Shorth to death with a stone. (*The Left Hand of Darkness*, p. 42)

Faxe, describing the function of the Weaver in a foretelling, explains what supposedly happened to Meshe:

> I serve as a filament, . . . The energy builds up and builds up in us, always sent
> back and back, redoubling the impulse every time until it breaks through and the light
> is in me, around me, I am the light. . . . The Old Man of Arbin Fastness once said that
> if the Weaver could be put in a vacuum at the moment of the Answer, he'd go on
> burning for years. That's what the Yomeshta believe of Meshe: that he saw past and
> future clear, not for a moment, but all during his life after the Question of Shorth.
> (*The Left Hand of Darkness*, p. 47)

Thus Meshe became omniscient, he knew all the answers that are of no consequence to the Handdarata, who prefer the Taoist ignorance. The Yomeshta, however, believe in knowledge and eternal light, and deny the existence of darkness as the source of all being. The beautifully conceived piece of the Yomeshta canon, "On Time and Darkness" (*The Left Hand of Darkness*, pp. 113-115) exemplifies the beliefs of the Yomeshta, their dogmatism, and the god-like position of Meshe as a centralized power:

> The life of every man is in the Center of Time, for all were seen in the Seeing of Meshe, and are in his Eye. We are the pupils of his Eye. Our doing is his Seeing: our being his knowing. (*The Left Hand of Darkness*, p. 114)

> There is neither darkness nor death, for all things are, in the light of the Moment, and their end and their beginning are one.
> One center, one seeing, one law, one light. Look now into the Eye of Meshe! (*The Left Hand of Darkness*, p. 115)

Considering LeGuin's interest in anthropology, it is interesting that anthropologists have discovered a sociological relationship between religion and society:

> It has long been realized that the ways in which a people order their social relationships are reflected in their concept of the supernatural and in their religious beliefs. This correspondence has led many observers to conclude that religious beliefs provide a legitimizing ideology which validates social organization and therefore helps to regulate social behavior.[43]

In a discussion of the fact that the Gethenians are the only mammalian and intelligent species on their planet, Genly tells Estraven that this is likely to affect their entire outlook. Estraven replies: "The Yomeshta would say that man's singularity is his divinity," and Genly Ai remarks:

> Lords of the Earth, yes. Other cults on other worlds have come to the same conclusion. They tend to be the cults of dynamic, aggressive, ecology-breaking cultures. Orgoreyn is in the pattern, in its way; at least they seem bent on pushing things around. (*The Left Hand of Darkness*, p. 163)

The anthropologist Vivelo states that a monotheistic form of religion or a tendency towards it is characteristic of a nation state:

> Since monotheism has obvious advantages for legitimizing central authority, it is not surprising that states - and those societies developing towards statedom - favor a monotheistic religion.[44]

The negatively rendered Orgoreyn endorses the monotheistic Yomesh cult, which basically postulates the same eternal present as the Handdara/Tao, only here it has become rigid and sterile through denying the creative duality of the

[43]Vivelo, *Cultural Anthropology Handbook*, p. 193.
[44]*ibid.*, p. 196.

Yin and Yang.[45] This break of the Handdarata/Taoist holistic vision enables Orgoreyn to threaten the planet for the first time with the possibility of war between two nations.

* * *

Karhide, the antidote to Orgoreyn, comes closer to being a future model for the androgynous psychology of humanity with its anarchic accumulation of (matriarchal) Clan-Hearths and a religion which features creative duality in unity. Orgoreyn, on the other hand, mirrors the modern Western industrialized state and its major religion, Christianity. The Yomesh cult and Christianity are parallel in that they both emerged from an older religion about two thousand years ago, that their founders are endowed with god-like qualities, that they both condemn darkness as evil, and that they consider human beings to be the "Lords of the Earth," thus providing the ground for an ideology of greed and exploitation of nature.[46]

The Handdara religion with its holistic outlook does not promote exploitation. Estraven says:

> Maybe [the Handdarata] are less aware of the gap between men and beasts, being more occupied with the likenesses, the links, the whole of which living things are part. (*The Left Hand of Darkness*, pp. 163-164)

The Handdara does not insist on a sterile unity, thus leaving space for the Other in the web of creation. The imagery of web and weaving is used in *The Left Hand of Darkness* in the foretelling where the Weaver weaves together the energies of disparate personalities and loosens them again because the ideal unity is never rigid and static but continually in motion, separating and reuniting. The metaphors of "web" and "weaving" are important and recurrent not only in the three novels under consideration here; they are often used in contemporary feminist utopian or speculative writing, usually standing for an ideal of community and/or the ecological unity of all living beings. LeGuin's inclusion of the temporal aspect in the Weaver's ritual function points to another interesting aspect of this metaphor, namely that it highlights the importance of invention and memory with regard to a utopian concept of the future: Invention in the sense of imagining something entirely novel and memory in the sense of a memory of the mythical Golden Age. In her study *Feminist Utopias*, Frances Bartkowski refers to Freud's discussion of the utopian impulse brought about by a present incident or situation arousing one of the subject's major wishes (present - dystopian condition to be criticized), then further developed by the subject's search in his or her memory for a moment when this wish was fulfilled (past, childhood - Golden Age), and finally resulting in a situation relating to the future in which this wish is fulfilled (utopia). Bartkowski remarks:

> The metaphor of weaving suggests these fictions [i.e. feminist utopian writing] as tapestries of an invented and remembered future. Where the unconscious is the

---

[45]See Bain, "The 'Tao te Ching' as Background," pp. 219-220. Cf. also N.B. Hayles, "Androgyny, Ambivalence and Assimilation in *The Left Hand of Darkness*," in *Ursula K. LeGuin*, ed. Olander and Greenberg, p. 101.
[46]Cf. Lake, "LeGuin's Twofold Vision," p. 160.

organizing agency of the dream of sleep and night, the ego, Freud specifies, is the hero of "every day-dream and every story."[47]

This is an interesting psychological aspect in the light of the orientation towards the past and the concurrent dreamlike qualities of the novels considered here - especially of *The Wanderground*, where the image of weaving is practically ubiquitous, and which is best read as a "dream world" and a "recreation of an unthreatening childhood world."[48]

* * *

Neither *Woman on the Edge of Time* nor *The Wanderground* feature institutionalized religions. Nevertheless, these novels emphasize strongly the need for a holistic world view as is implied in the Tao and which is expressed by the use of the web-imagery, too.

In Mattapoisett, the system of ecology is important. Human beings have to learn that they are part of the whole and cannot simply change or exploit things because it would affect the whole - an attitude which determines scientific research, among other things. There is not, however, a fixed system of beliefs that can be taught, such as we usually associate with religion. In order to achieve a sense of unity with nature and the environment, the people practice "inknowing". The utopian people in *Woman on the Edge of Time* have taken from all cultures what they consider to be useful, but they have not created a religion as such because everybody has to develop freely and fully without dogmatic interference. Luciente tells Connie: "You might say our - you'd say religion? - ideas make us see ourselves as partners with water, air, birds, fish, trees." (*Woman on the Edge of Time*, p. 125) When they talk about death and burial, Luciente tells Connie:

> Connie, your old way appears barbaric to us, trying to keep the rotting body. To pretend we are not made of elements as ancient as the earth, that we do not owe those elements back to the web of all living . . . (*Woman on the Edge of Time*, p. 162)

Dying, in Mattapoisett, is called "giving back." This feeling of being part of all life is not caused by the belief in a transcendental cosmic force, such as the Tao is. Instead, the natural life-style in Piercy's utopia supposedly leads automatically to this end:

> Connie, we are born screaming Ow and I! The gift is in growing to care, to connect, to cooperate. Everything we learn aims to make us feel strong in ourselves, connected to all living. At home. (*Woman on the Edge of Time*, p. 248)

Piercy obviously assumes that a harmonious life in a healthy environment will make religion superfluous. People in tune with their environment will be happy and do not fear death because it, too, belongs to the eternal cycle of life. The holistic world view of Piercy's utopian conception allows for communication with animals based on sign language and behaviorism, because animals are valuable parts of the "web of all living." (*Woman on the Edge of Time*, p. 98) Healing

---

[47] Frances Bartkowski, *Feminist Utopias* (Lincoln and London: University of Nebraska Press, 1989) p. 11.
[48] Cf. Lefanu's reading of *The Wanderground* in part 2.3.

94

methods include mystical forces but are not explained in any detail, and dreams determine who may speak for the Earth and the animals.

* * *

In *The Wanderground*, this connection between the women and nature is most strongly expressed by the spiritual link between the women, plants, animals, and the elements. The discussion of *The Wanderground* in part 2.3 has shown that Gearhart draws considerably on ancient religions, mysticism, and esoterics. The elements of these in *The Wanderground*, however, do not assemble into a new religion. The idea of religion, a doctrine or even a deity contradicts the anarchic concept of the Wanderground. Old Artilidea, being angry because a tempest destroyed half of the ensconcement's winter grain, curses the "Goddess". This stuns the young girl Voki: "You cursed the Goddess?" Artilidea answers: "The Goddess? Well, of course. Such as she is," and then asks Voki: "Who's been dosing you up on reverence?" She then explains to the puzzled girl: "I'm cursing our own closedness, Voki. We should have known, could have cut and gathered sooner." (*The Wanderground*, p. 184) The required openness is explained by old Pelagine who remembers the beginnings of the Wanderground:

> Hard work learning new ways, hard work learning new skills. . . . Understanding the out-of-doors - things about wood and fire, rivers and dirt, wind and weather. Learning to listen to what the land wants you to do and still keeping your ears open while you do it. (*The Wanderground*, p. 79)

Openness and receptivity are valued highly among the women - Taoist virtues, at which Gearhart also oriented her alternative world. Betha, on rotation in the city, recites from the *I Ching*: "Tui, . . . the lake on the lake, female on female." (*The Wanderground*, p. 115) Tui, the sign of the two lakes, is a feminine sign of the *I Ching*:

> A lake evaporates and thus empties itself slowly. If, however, two lakes are connected to one another, they cannot easily be drained, because one enriches the other.[49]

Gearhart has interpreted this image with regard to communication: "Meaningful communication is the meeting of two vessels, equally vulnerable, equally receptive, equally desirous of hearing. In the listening is all real speaking." (*The Wanderground*, p. 115) The "Regard of Tui" is also based on this sign:

> Tui. A moment of hope for agreement . . . Some unity, some bonding on a fundamental level struck an ultimate sense in every gatherstretching woman . . . All leaned together toward the image of woman-on-woman, women-on-women, toward the sameness and toward the differences that mark any two or any two thousand women. All moved toward the gentle holding of two calm lakes, each one of the other. (*The Wanderground*, p. 129)

---

[49]Wilhelm, Richard, trans. *I Ging, Text und Materialien* (Köln: Diederichs, Gelbe Reihe, 1973) p. 212. In choosing to translate from this edition/translation, the same reasons as given in note 35 apply.

This openness and receptivity opens the way to every woman's intrapersonal energy flow, which will allow her the fruitful use of an interpersonal energy, connecting her to the world and to all beings. In equating "Goddess" with the women themselves, Artilidea expresses the idea that everything which is considered divine or worthy of reverence today is really located in one's own self, that this is our own intra- and interpersonal energy. The connection between the presence of the hill women and their energy in the cities, where it helps to contain the destructive male energy, and the effect of the "Revolt of the Earth", intimates that this revolt is indeed the result of the combined energy of women who became "too wide awake, i.e. politically conscious. (*The Wanderground*, p. 145) The "Revolt of the Earth" occurs after large numbers of women left the cities, and it occurs when some of these women have daydreams which prefigure it (see *The Wanderground*, pp. 158-160). Moreover, the women create the presence of the Earth and its voice by their own "channel-joining" (telepathic linking of minds, *The Wanderground*, pp. 192-193). Thus, Gearhart's "*dea ex machina*" would be the result of her favored strategy of feminism: energy-resourcement.

* * *

Gearhart locates the source of personal strength and integrity in the women's selves. The earth as mother becomes their source and origin. This resembles the idea of the Tao, but Gearhart stripped it of its transcendental aspect, thus altering the concept of the Tao substantially. The cycle of life takes place on earth, and any form of energy is created by its material aspects and by its living beings; no other supernatural beings or levels of existence are involved. As in Piercy's Mattapoisett, a natural life in tune with one's environment, and a free and full development will enable the women to grow their special skills and to feel part of the whole world. Their expression for dying is "to change form" (*The Wanderground*, p. 13), which carries the same connotations as Piercy's "to give back". The hill women feel when they are ready to die, and they die of their own will, just as the inhabitants of Mattapoisett do. Another parallel between *The Wanderground* and *Woman on the Edge of Time* is the importance of celebrations and rituals. The hill women have special ceremonies for egg-implantments (artificial reproduction impregnation) and for ovulation which, in miraculous uniformity, occurs to all women simultaneously in tune with the lunar cycle. The celebration of the menstrual cycle as part of the cycle of all life exemplifies the value of women and their exclusive experiences in a feminocentric society. Furthermore, there are ceremonies for dying women, daily "twilight ministrations", the meaning and function of which is left unexplained, and many ritual sayings, rhymes, and incantations, which form the hill women's culture.

The women's telepathic and empathic skills can be read as metaphor for the women's unity with nature. They are always described as surrounding and receptive. Gearhart reinterprets the all-inclusiveness of the Tao as an all-encompassing receptivity (which is, however, actually only one half of the original concept of the Tao):

> We are built to receive. Let's say that loud and clear. We are also built to give, but even our giving is in our own mode and that mode is totally different from that mis-sourced *inter*personal energy exercised by most men (and unfortunately by many women). Instead of probing or invading, our natural giving takes the form of wrapping around the givee, of being available to her/him without insisting; our giving is a

presence, an *offering*, an *opening*, a *surrounding*, a *listening*, a *vulnerability*, a *trust*. At the very most our giving takes the form of a push toward freedom for the givee, as in the act of *giving* birth.

So in reclaiming our bodies, let's also affirm some propaganda: We are what our fathers and husbands . . . have called us, but what they have not known, or what they knew and suppressed because of its potential paralyzing threat, is that in our listening is all meaning, in our vesseling is the home, . . ., in our nurturing is all possibility. In our enfolding, in short, is all power. But in the force and thrust of renegade and exclusive *inter*personal (. . .) energy, there can only be havoc and destruction.[50]

Gearhart thus regards women to be the source of all creative forces; they become the force of her transformed Tao. Due to her assumption of men's different nature and the defects of the male psyche, Gearhart does not believe that their psychic powers may be benevolent. Evona mistrusts the Gentles because they do not "enfold" their partner but build a telepathic "bridge", i.e. a linear way, which Evona equates with a sword and "a fancy prick to invade the world with." (*The Wanderground*, p. 179)

* * *

LeGuin also uses telepathy as a symbol for connection, understanding, and wholeness, in *The Left Hand of Darkness*. Genly Ai and the people of the Ekumen possess the skill of "mindspeech", i.e. telepathic communication in verbal form. It is a teachable skill which requires a certain stage of development:

[E]xcept in the case of the born Sensitive, the capacity, though it has a physiological basis, is a psychological one, a product of culture, a side effect of the use of the mind. Young children, and defectives, and members of unevolved or regressed societies, can't mindspeak. The mind must exist on a certain plane of complexitiy first. . . . Abstract thought, varied social interaction, intricate cultural adjustments, esthetic and ethical perception, all of this has to reach a certain level before the connection can be made - before the potentiality can be touched at all. (*The Left Hand of Darkness*, p. 175)

These prerequisites do not conform to the Tao doctrine of ignorance, of a return to a simple and natural life style. In using telepathy as a metaphor for the ability to connect, however, it may indicate the spiritual and intellectual growth of Genly Ai. As long as he remained a dualist thinker, believing in either-or logic, clinging to his masculinity, he was excluded from Estraven's androgynous world:

A friend. What is a friend in a world where any friend may be a lover at a new phase of the moon? Not I, locked in my virility: no friend to Therem Harth, or any other of his race. (*The Left Hand of Darkness*, p. 149)

Only after he has been able to accept Estraven's female/feminine aspect, too, and thus finally accepts him as an androgyne, Genly Ai is able to establish mindspeech with him. It is the metaphor for their ultimate love and understanding.

* * *

---

[50]Gearhart, "Womanpower," p. 198.

The areas of religion and mysticism are most intricately elaborated in *The Left Hand of Darkness*. LeGuin, using her anthropological method, has applied concepts of existing religions to her imaginary societies with considerable skill and consistency, effectively underlining her other themes with them.

Piercy did not give much care to these areas at all. Her people are not really mystics since the "mystical" practices of the people of Mattapoisett are no longer mysterious to us (e.g. meditation, yoga). The only exception are the - unfortunately unexplained - healing techniques.

The Wanderground uses parapsychological and mystical skills most extensively but rejects any form of religion. Gearhart radically transforms the Tao in stripping it of its mystical and transcendental aspects, thus giving primacy to immediate physical and sensual experience and existence. The "religious" attitude of the hill women is animistic, regarding every being as being endowed with the same spiritual dimension that they themselves possess, since they are all part of the same world. Thus, in all three novels, religion and mysticism are intended to emphasize the unity of humanity and nature, and the necessity to acknowledge that humanity is not the crown of creation, but only one of its many parts.

3.4 Language

Let me conclude the comparison of certain aspects of the imaginary societies in *The Left Hand of Darkness*, *Woman on the Edge of Time* and *The Wanderground* with a short survey of the use of language modification as a means to underline in what way these societal conceptions differ from the author's own societies.

* * *

LeGuin presents the reader with a different planet. She thus implies the existence of different languages (Karhidish, Orgota), but the language in which she writes must be understood by the reader.[51] In *The Left Hand of Darkness*, certain words and concepts are given in Karhidish and Orgota, such as "shifgrethor", the difficult game of prestige establishment, or various words for different kinds of snow and ice, which is important in the Gethenian glacial climate. This evokes the famous example of the Eskimo language which possesses a range of expressions for what the ordinary English speaker would call snow. LeGuin obviously draws upon the theory of linguistic determinism in its weakened form, namely that a language influences the perception of the environment, but does not determine it completely.

The Terran Genly Ai has been transposed into an alien world which he has to describe in English. He has to face the problem of translation, and in the context of this study it is important that he has to deal with a significant lexical gap of the English language: it does not possess a generic pronoun for "he/she" for an androgyne (or hermaphrodite). The Investigator Ong Tot Oppong delineates this problem and its implications:

> [Y]ou cannot think of a Gethenian as "it". They are not neuters . . .. Lacking the Karhidish "human pronoun" used for persons in somer, I must say "he," for the same

---

[51]Cf. Victoria Myers, "Conversational Technique in Ursula LeGuin: A Speech-Act Analysis," *Science Fiction Studies*, 10 (1983) p. 306.

reasons as we used the masculine pronoun in referring to a transcendent god: it is less defined, less specific, than the neuter or the feminine. But the very use of the pronoun in my thoughts leads me continually to forget that the Karhider I am with is not a man, but a manwoman. (*The Left Hand of Darkness*, p. 66)

LeGuin justifies the use of the pronoun "he" for a Gethenian: "I call Gethenians 'he,' because I utterly refuse to mangle English by inventing a pronoun for 'he/she.' 'He' is the generic pronoun, damn it, in English."[52] LeGuin has been repeatedly criticized for this decision, as for example by Rhodes:

> While LeGuin is not to be faulted for her grammar, one must consider whether as an artist her obligation is to grammar or to producing more valid results from her fictional thought-experiment. If as an artist she can invent a new futuristic world with new religions and new cultural groupings, then, can't she invent new words to depict accurately her vision of the androgyne?[53]

Rhodes infers: "A human and androgyne are not one and the same; language should make the difference clear."[54] A man (Genly Ai) and an androgyne are not the same, but a human might well be androgynous. The Gethenian languages do have different pronouns for a "kemmerer" (a Gethenian in kemmer) who has become male, for one who has become female, for "generic human", and even for a male animal and a female animal (these are used for "perverts", i.e. Gethenians who, either because of a physiological defect or due to hormonal treatment, are continually in kemmer as male or female; cf. *The Left Hand of Darkness*, p. 44). Genly Ai, however, tells his story in English, not in Karhidish or Orgota. Moreover, the point at issue is not necessarily one of accurate distinction and denomination, but one of culturally determined and linguistically influenced perception, which may under certain circumstances be limited. Rhodes, in her

---

[52]LeGuin, "Is Gender Necessary?" p. 168. Feminist linguists, however, have demonstrated that "he" as generic pronoun is unfit to serve its function. See, for example, Wendy Martyna, "Beyond the 'He/Man' Approach: The Case for Nonsexist Language," *Signs*, 5 (1980) pp. 482-493; Janice Moulton *et al.*, "Sex Bias in Language Use: Neutral Pronouns That Aren't," *American Psychologist*, 33,11 (1978) pp. 1032-1036; Senta Trömel-Plötz, "Sexismus in der Englischen Sprache," *Englisch-Amerikanische Studien*, 2 (1989) pp. 189-204. LeGuin herself admits this fully in the new version of "Is Gender Necessary?": "I still dislike invented pronouns, but I now like them better than the so-called generic pronoun he/him/his, which does in fact exclude women from discourse; and which was an invention of male grammarians, for until the seventh century the English generic singular pronoun was they/them/their, as it still is in English and American colloquial speech." (*Dancing at the Edge of the World*, p. 15) For a screenplay of *The Left Hand of Darkness*, written in 1985, she has invented pronouns for Gethenians not pregnant or in kemmer. (*ibid.*)
[53]Rhodes, "Ursula LeGuin's *The Left Hand of Darkness*," p. 115.
[54]*ibid.*, p. 116. LeGuin took this criticism to heart as early as 1975, before she revised her opinion expressed in the original "Is Gender Necessary?" She revised the short story "Winter's King", written a year before *The Left Hand of Darkness* and also about Gethen. She had used the "generic he" originally, but in revising the story for the short story collection *The Wind's Twelve Quarters* in 1975 she "saw a chance to redress that injustice slightly. In this version, I use the feminine pronoun for all Gethenians - while preserving certain masculine titles such as King and Lord, just to remind one of the ambiguity. This may drive some nonfeminists mad, but that's only fair." (Ursula K. LeGuin, "Winter's King", in *The Wind's Twelve Quarters*, pp. 75-95. See the preface, p. 75.) "Winter's King", however, does not thematize androgyny, or gender role stereotypes. Therefore, LeGuin's linguistic revision here remains an entertaining but ultimately unimportant side-effect.

criticism, completely overlooks the fact that LeGuin's usage of the "generic he" reveals our culturally conditioned gender-determined perception. For us, it is difficult to really comprehend an androgynous/hermaphroditic nature. Genly Ai exemplifies this:

> Though I had been nearly two years on Winter I was still far from being able to see the people of the planet through their own eyes. I tried to, but my efforts took the form of self-consciously seeing a Gethenian first as a man, then as a woman, forcing him into these categories so irrelevant to his nature and so essential to my own . . . I thought that at table Estraven's performance had been womanly, all charm and tact and lack of substance, specious and adroit. Was it in fact this soft supple femininity that I disliked and distrusted in him? For it was impossible to think of him as a woman, that dark, ironic powerful presence near me in the firelit darkness, and yet whenever I thought of him as a man, I felt a sense of falseness, of imposture: in him, or in my own attitude towards him? (*The Left Hand of Darkness*, pp. 8-9)

Genly is culturally conditioned to think in binary oppositions. He is actually sexist, presuming fixed categories for feminine and masculine attributes. On Gethen, however, he is continually confused: His motherly, feminine "landlady" has never been a mother and "[t]he king was pregnant." (*The Left Hand of Darkness*, p. 69) LeGuin herself admitted that if she had used this method more extensively, she would have been more successful at keeping Gethenian androgyny/hermaphroditism in the reader's mind:

> The pronouns wouldn't matter at all if I had been cleverer at *showing* the "female" component of the Gethenian characters in *action*. [*If I had realized how the pronouns I used shaped, directed, controlled my own thinking, I might have been "cleverer."*][55]

Estraven is mostly shown in male roles, but when his feminine aspects surface, they puzzle Genly Ai. After getting to know Estraven better, Genly Ai realizes that his own thinking is dichotomous and that the same thing may be called by a different name when done by a man or a woman: Estraven's meticulous food-ration calculations can be seen as "either housewifely or scientific," (*The Left Hand of Darkness*, pp. 168-169) depending on whether he is perceived as feminine or masculine respectively. This, too, belongs to the problem of perceiving, and linguistically classifying, an androgyne/hermaphrodite. Genly Ai is the point of identification for the reader in confronting the Gethenians. Gisela Ecker remarks:

> LeGuin's argument that this utopian [sic] world is presented through the perspective of a narrator of the "old patriarchal world", who necessarily has to use his language with its specific conceptualizations might help us to understand the novel but does not reduce our uneasiness when reading it.[56]

In my opinion, the "uneasiness" felt by Ecker is not LeGuin's fault. The shortcomings are in the English language: If we encountered a hermaphroditic/androgynous living being, we would have no pronoun to refer to it. Genly Ai has no other choice than using "he". This is what ought to be the cause of Ecker's uneasiness: Sexism is inscribed into the English language and

---

[55] LeGuin, *Dancing at the Edge of the World*, p. 15. Cf. also 3.1.
[56] Ecker, "The Politics of Fantasy," p. 507.

therefore also into the readers' culture and into their minds - as LeGuin herself exemplifies (see quotation above). LeGuin does not write about the future but about the present, and at present the English language contains sexist elements which obscur that - according to LeGuin - human beings are really psychologically androgynous.

* * *

Piercy approached the problem from the angle suggested by Rhodes and Ecker because Mattapoisett is a future conception of a society. Piercy's utopian people have eclipsed sexual oppression. Since not only language influences thinking, but perception can also shape language (codability), the future inhabitants of Piercy's utopia do not distinguish pronominally between the sexes. "He", "she", "his", "her", "him", and so forth are all replaced by "person" or "per". This simple device, together with using words like "chairperson" instead of "chairman", has an overwhelming effect.

It is interesting to note that a similar reform of language has actually occured in the community of "Twin Oaks" in the U.S.A. where the people use "co" instead of "he" or "she".[57] "Twin Oaks", which was originally modelled on Skinner's *Walden II*, has many parallels to Mattapoisett, thus conforming Piercy's claim to have created a "practical utopia": a communal life style which dissolved domestic work, a credit system for labor which replaced the monetary (capitalist) system, the rotation of jobs with the aim to break gender stereotypes, and communal decisions about how many births can be afforded (pregnancy is considered labor and earns credits). There are spiritual activities, and people may change their names as an act of consciousness-raising. In Mattapoisett, people can change their names whenever they feel that they have changed. This right is an expression of the self, of its continual growth and transformation. Connie is puzzled by this possibility, because in her culture names serve as means of bureaucratic indentification and control. Furthermore, in the case of a married woman, it indicates the "change of possession" from father to husband.

> Look, my name is Consuelo Ramos. Connie for short. Consuelo is my Christian name, my first name. Ramos is my last name. When I was born I was called Consuelo Camacho. Ramos is the name of my second husband: Therefore I am Consuelo Camacho Ramos. (*Woman on the Edge of Time*, p. 76)

* * *

In *The Wanderground*, the hill women also choose their individual names. (*The Wanderground*, p. 73) Monique Wittig writes of her women in *Les Guérillères*, a precursor of *The Wanderground* in the tradition of all-female societies maintaining themselves against patriarchal enemies:

> THAT WHICH IDENTIFIES THEM LIKE
> THE EYE OF THE CYCLOPS,
> THEIR SINGLE FORENAME,

---

[57] For this discussion of "Twin Oaks", see Weinbaum, "Twin Oaks."

OSEA BALKIS SARA NICEA
IOLA CORA SABINA DANIELA
GALSWINTHA EDNA JOSEPHA [58]

Wittig continues this litany of women's names from myths and from all cultures and languages throughout her book, interspersing them on every third page. Gearhart's women choose similar names, and have only one, i.e. they are possessed by nobody else but themselves.

In *Les Guérillères*, Wittig devoted some paragraphs to the relationship of women and language in a patriarchy. Her women accuse men of having "attached a particular word to an object or a fact and thereby consider themselves to have appropriated it."[59] As a consequence

> the language you speak is made up of signs that rightly speaking designate what men have appropriated. Whatever they have not laid hands on, whatever they have not pounced on like many-eyed birds of prey, does not appear in the language you speak. This is apparent precisely in the intervals that your masters have not been able to fill with their words of proprietors and possessors, this can be found in the gaps, in all that which is not a continuation of their discourse, in the zero, the O, the perfect circle that you invent to overthrow them.[60]

The gaps in the "masters' language", which could not be claimed by them, may be interpreted as female experiences and abilities. Gearhart has filled them in *The Wanderground* with numerous terms for what she has called "Womanpower". Women, in Gearhart's opinion, are in the possession of fruitful intra- and interpersonal energies. In *The Wanderground*, these take the form of empathy, telepathy, and other parapsychological skills. All of these have to be named, which defamiliarizes the language of the hill women: they have created a culture which is different from the reader's, therefore their language is also different. The difference is mainly in the vocabulary. There are hardly any words for technological artefacts, but innumerous terms for mental skills, some of which render technology superfluous. The category of a kind of mental radar with which the women check their environment comprises terms like "listenspread", "extended ear", fan-spread", and so on. The words for telepathic and emphatic communication include a vast variation of "stretches", "channel-joining", "enfoldments", "enwombings", and so forth. The women have "hard selves", i.e. physical bodies, and several levels of spiritual existences called "soft self", "lonth" and so on, which are, however, animistic (i.e. they will also die when the woman dies). The importance of the considerable body of vocabulary for the distinction between and determination of communication and feelings lies in the implication of the high value of these areas of personal experience and human interaction in the Wanderground society. The present-day rationalist Western culture is juxtaposed to a utopian society which values feelings, instincts, and loving interaction. Gearhart's overextensive use of the terminology for mental skills, however, alienates the reader and renders *The Wanderground* overly fantastic.

The problem of sexism in contemporary English is not topicalized in *The Wanderground*. Since there are no men, the hill women use a "generic" she.

---

[58] Monique Wittig, *Les Guérillères* (1969), trans. David Le Vay (New York: Bard/Avon, 1973) p. 13.
[59] *ibid.*, p. 114.
[60] *ibid.*

Since Wittig's *Les Guérillères*, language has become a subject of increasing importance for feminist writers of utopian fiction and science fiction. In her novel *From the Legend of Biel* (1975), Mary Staton expresses a view of present-day languages similar to Wittig's, calling them the "syntax of despair":

> [T]hese ill people spoke of owning each other, of owning land, ideas, animals, everything. They permitted governments and systems to try and control nonexistent entities like The People, Education, Health, even Death. They could not seem to understand that it is impossible to own mates, progeny, land, knowledge or emotions.[61]

In 1984 Suzette Haden Elgin published her novel *Native Tongue*, which is set in the year 2179, when men reign supreme on Earth and its colonized planets, and women are barred from all power. As a means of resistance, the women develop their own secret language, called Láadan. This language, just like the hill women's one, places considerable emphasis on its vocabulary for feelings and sensations. By comparison, present-day English is rather underdeveloped in this area.

This increasing interest in language in modern women's writing is directly related to the topicalization of sexism in language by contemporary feminist theory and the new field of feminist linguistics.[62] The novels examined here reflect some of the major concerns raised by feminist theory and linguistics: *The Left Hand of Darkness* points to the inadequacy and limitations of a language which contains sexist elements. *Woman on the Edge of Time* and *The Wanderground* suggest possible solutions, or, at least, improvements - the former by suggesting reforms in the structure of language, the latter in emphasizing the importance of reclaiming and inventing words and expressions which denote women's exclusive experiences and (female) mental capacities.

[61]Mary Staton, *From the Legend of Biel* (New York: Ace, 1975) p. 176.

[62]See Mary Daly, *Gyn/Ecology* (1975), as an early thematization of re-appropriating language from the patriarchy. See also *Women and Language in Literature and Society*, McConnell-Ginet *et al.*, eds. (New York: Praeger, 1980), and the works of Wendy Martyna and Cheris Kramarae.

4. CONCLUSION

In Wittig's novel *Les Guérillères*, a woman appeals:

> There was a time when you were not a slave, remember that. You walked alone, full of laughter, you bathed bare-bellied. You say you have lost all recollection of it, remember. The wild roses in the woods. Your hand is torn on the bushes gathering mulberries and strawberries you refresh yourself with . . .. You say there are no words to describe this time, you say it does not exist. But remember. Make an effort to remember. Or, failing that, invent.[1]

This programmatic call for women to imagine a utopia in which they are free and independent points to the psychological importance of women's ability to do so: it will inevitably enhance their self-confidence and self-assurance (cf. Göttner-Abendroth on matriarchy in 2.2 and Russ on the ability to imagine all-women worlds at the end of 2.3).

In 1973, Joanna Russ wrote "What Can a Heroine Do? or Why Women Can't Write", a witty and polemical essay about the problems faced by women writers in a patriarchal culture who want to write about female protagonists.[2] Their options, Russ wrote, are very limited because the patriarchal male culture allows women only few restricted roles and denies the importance and often the existence of their specific experiences. At the end of her essay, Russ observed that some literary genres offer loopholes through which the women writer may escape the heavy weight of patriarchally prescribed myths on her writing; one of these genres is science fiction.

* * *

The Women's Movement and the feminist discourse have had their impact on society. The critique of and fight against the oppression of women have entailed legal reforms and a consciousness raising among women (and some men as well) which widened their options and prospects.

Feminism and the Women's Movement have also provided the tradition and community which hold and share certain beliefs necessary for women writers to use the utopian mode - the literary genre *par excellence* to explore a wider variety of life styles and a broader range of possibilities. As the latter became available for women in their society, too, women writers could appropriate the utopian mode which nowadays appears almost exclusively in science fiction, long after the male-dominated mainstream literature has almost completely abandoned it.

---

[1] Wittig, *Les Guérillères*, p. 89.

[2] Joanna Russ, "What Can a Heroine Do? or Why Women Can't Write," in *Images of Women in Fiction: Feminist Perspectives*, S. Koppelman Cornillon, ed.(Bowling Green, Ohio: Bowling Green State University Popular Press, 1973) pp. 3-20.

Most utopian writing by women is past oriented, evoking "memories" of matriarchs, amazons, witches, powerful women of the past, and proposing the reversion to a simpler life style.[3]

The Left Hand of Darkness, Woman on the Edge of Time, and *The Wanderground* all imply a critique of the contemporary belief in unlimited progress and of a hypertrophied technology which threatens the ecological equilibrium of the earth. *Woman on the Edge of Time* and *The Left Hand of Darkness*, however, opt for a limited and careful use of technology in their conceptions of future societies.

The general orientation towards a past societal stage in women's utopian writing is not only due to a "memory" of the "Golden Age", a belief that things could not always have been so bad for women. It is rather the fictional complement to that branch of feminist analysis which tries to find the roots of and the cause for the patriarchal system. The resulting maxime, in simplified form, is to go back to where it started, and begin afresh. That is, in future terms: to reduce exploitative technology, and to reform the inequality between the sexes.

* * *

The suggestions and solutions offered by women's utopian writing today are numerous and of considerable variety. In *The Left Hand of Darkness*, LeGuin proposes that the full realization of psychological androgyny will improve society, but she does not offer any concrete suggestions as to how androgyny can be achieved on the societal plane. Instead, she implies in *The Left Hand of Darkness* that it must be realized on the personal plane first. This is why Genly Ai is able to realize his own androgyny when he is isolated with Estraven on the Gobrin Ice.

As long as Genly Ai was confined to his masculinity, women were alien and incomprehensible to him (see *The Left Hand of Darkness*, p. 164), but when he accepts the androgynous Estraven and, consequently, his own feminine aspects, he perceives the shared qualities of all human beings, the links between them. In short, he realizes that sex does not naturally entail gender. LeGuin believes that the "circle, the true society, is formed of single bodies and single souls. If not, it is not formed at all."[4] Consciousness raising must occur in the individual before it can affect societal change.

Piercy holds a similar view but emphasizes the need for collective action after the individual consciousness raising process:

> It goes on one at a time,
> it starts when you care
> to act, it starts when you do
> it again after they said no,
> it starts when you say *We*
> and know who you mean, and each
> day you mean one more.[5]

---

[3]A noteworthy exception is Mary Staton's *From the Legend of Biel*, which also features artificial reproduction similar to *Woman on the Edge of Time*, and a highly complex but benevolent technology.

[4]Ursula K. LeGuin, "Science Fiction and Mrs. Brown," in *The Language of the Night*, p. 117. Originally published in *Science Fiction at Large*, P. Nicholls, ed. (New York: Harper & Row, 1976).

[5]Marge Piercy, from "The Low Road," in *The Moon is Always Female: Poems by Marge Piercy* (New York: Alfred A. Knopf, 1982) pp. 44-45.

In her novel *Woman on the Edge of Time*, the utopian society of Mattapoisett is not discontinuous with contemporary society, but a possible extension of it, created by people who became politically active. Curiously, Mattapoisett seems to exist simultaneously with the present for which it is an alternative. This led many critics to wonder whether it is only a hallucination of the despairing Connie. This question, however, is irrelevant. Piercy's message is that political action is based on a utopian vision. Connie's ability to imagine a better world, a world in which she would be valued, renders her self-confident, and she feels obliged to fight for her utopian vision in spite of her own utter powerlessness. The end of the novel, however, is ambiguous. Mattapoisett is rendered as a possible and practicable society, but Connie's action, the murder of her doctors, will be of no real consequence - other doctors will continue the research. Connie cannot start a movement or be united with one. One person alone can raise her or his own consciousness, but cannot change society.[6]

* * *

Gearhart calls for a collective movement in both her novel *The Wanderground* as well as in her essays. The Radical Lesbian Separatism promoted in *The Wanderground* is the most provocative suggestion. It is actually followed by many American women who live on women's farms in the country. Batya Weinbaum considers them to be

> centers for cultural and psychic development, to which women can come to cleanse themselves of male, negative, and city energies; and to be exposed to new thinking and psychic phenomena.[7]

Gearhart's views are extreme: women are hopelessly victimized in a patriarchal society, and she does not see any alternative to separatism, which, however, excludes most women (non-lesbians) as they do not regard it to be a possibility for themselves. Moreover, Gearhart's biologism is controversial, and it is disturbing that she seems to believe that men are innately and unalterably violent: "It is not in his nature not to rape. It is not in my nature to be raped. We do not co-exist." (The *Wanderground*, p. 25) This final condemnation of men, without any indication that at some point in the future the sexes may live harmoniously together, leaves the reader with strongly equivocal feelings.

* * *

The Left Hand of Darkness, Woman on the Edge of Time, The Wanderground, and many other writings in the utopian mode by women writers share common concerns such as gender equality, reproduction, sexuality, ecology, a holistic world view, and often a reversion to a simpler life style. There are, however, various ways to approach these, and various proposals for solutions.

---

[6]Cf. "The Low Road," *ibid.*, p. 44: "What can they do/ to you? Whatever they want./ They can set you up, they can/ bust you, they can break/ your fingers, they can/ burn your brain with electricity,/ blur you with drugs till you/ can't walk, can't remember, they can/ take your child, wall up/ your lover. They can do anything/ you can't stop them/ from doing. How can you stop/ them? Alone, you can fight,/ you can refuse, you can/ take what revenge you can/ but they roll over you."
[7]Weinbaum, "Twin Oaks," pp. 157-158.

In general, there exists a fruitful reciprocity between feminist theory and feminist utopian writing. If the literary critic does not take this into account, he/she may overlook that the emphasis is on the conceptualization of new ideas and not on innovation or originality in the aesthetic and literary area. On the other hand, the feminist critic must be careful not to measure women's utopias against her own political stance since a work of fiction is not a political tract. Piercy's omission to fully explain the necessity of artificial reproduction in *Woman on the Edge of Time*, for instance, is not an aesthetical flaw because the story remains consistent. Feminist utopian conceptions of future societies are a playground on which different ideas and models can be tested in an entertaining and thought-stimulating way - the wide range of feminist utopian writing testifies to this.

BIBLIOGRAPHY

A. Primary Literature

Atwood, Margaret. *The Handmaid's Tale*. Toronto: McClelland and Steward, 1985.

Bacon, Francis. *New Atlantis* (1621). Rpt. in *The Works of Francis Bacon*, vol. II. Ed. James Spedding, Robert L. Ellis, and Douglas D. Heath. London: Longman's & Co. *et al.*, 1870, pp. 123-166.

Bellamy, Edward. *Looking Backward* (1880). Rpt. Ed. Cecelia Tichi. Harmondsworth: Penguin, 1982.

Bradley, Marion Zimmer. *The Ruins of Isis*. New York: Pocket Books, 1979.

Callenbach, Ernest. *Ecotopia: A Novel about Ecology, People and Politics in 1999* (1975). London: Pluto Press, 1978.

Charnas, Suzy McKee. *Walk to the End of the World*. New York: Ballantine Books, 1974.

-----. *Motherlines*. New York: Berkeley/Putnam, 1978.

Corbett, Mrs. George [Elizabeth Burgoyne Corbett]. *New Amazonia: A Foretaste of the Future*. London: Tower Publishing Co., 1889.

Elgin, Suzette Haden. *Native Tongue*. New York: Daw Books, 1984.

Gearhart, Sally Miller. *The Wanderground: Stories of the Hill Women*. Watertown, Mass.: Persephone Press, 1979.

Gilman, Charlotte Perkins. *Herland* (1915). Rpt. London: The Women's Press, 1986.

Huxley, Aldous. *Brave New World* (1932). Rpt. London: Triad/Panther Books, 1977.

[Jones, Alice Ilgenfritz, and Ella Merchant.] *Unveiling a Parallel: A Romance*, by Two Women of the West (pseud.). Boston: Arena Publishing Co., 1893.

Lane, Mary E. Bradley. *Mizora: A Prophecy* (1880-1881). Rpt. Boston: Gregg Press, G.K. Hall, 1975.

LeGuin, Ursula K. *The Left Hand of Darkness*. New York: Harper & Row, 1969.

-----. *The Dispossessed*. New York: Harper & Row, 1974.

-----."Winter's King." In *The Wind's Twelve Quarters: Short Stories by Ursula K. LeGuin*. New York: Harper & Row, 1975, pp. 75-95.

More, Thomas. *Utopia* (1516). Rpt. Harmondsworth: Penguin, 1961.

Morris, William. *News From Nowhere* (1890). Rpt. Ed. Asa Briggs. Harmondsworth: Penguin, 1984.

Orwell, George. *Nineteen Eighty-Four* (1949). Rpt. Harmondsworth: Penguin, 1954.

Phelps, Elizabeth Stuart. *The Gates Ajar* (1868). Rpt. Cambridge, Mass.: Harvard University Press, 1964.

-----. *Beyond the Gates*. Boston: Houghton Mifflin Co., 1883.

-----. *The Gates Between*. Boston: Houghton Mifflin Co., 1887.

Piercy, Marge. *Small Changes*. New York: Doubleday, 1973.

-----. *Woman on the Edge of Time*. New York: Fawcett Crest, 1976.

-----."The Low Road." In *The Moon is Always Female: Poems by Marge Piercy*. New York: Alfred A. Knopf, 1982, pp. 44-45.

Plato. *Essays*. Vol. II: *The Republic*. New York: Arno, 1894.

Russ, Joanna. *The Female Man*. New York: Bantam, 1975.

Scott, Sarah Robinson. *A Description of Millenium Hall and the Country Adjacent* (1762). Rpt. London: Virago Press, 1986.

Staton, Mary. *From the Legend of Biel*. New York: Ace, 1975.

Sturgeon, Theodore. *Venus Plus X*. New York: Pyramid Books, 1960.

Wells, Herbert G. *A Modern Utopia* (1905). In *Tono Bungay and A Modern Utopia*. London: Odhams Press Ltd., n.d.

Wittig, Monique. *Les Guérillères* (1969). Trans. David Le Vay. New York: Bard/Avon, 1973.

Wyndham, John. *Consider Her Ways*. New York: Ballantine Books, 1956.

B. Secondary Literature

Adler, Margot. "Meanings of Matriarchy." In *The Politics of Women's Spirituality*. Ed. Charlene Spretnak. Garden City, N.Y.: Anchor/Doubleday, 1982, pp. 127-137.

Amrain, Susanne. "Der Androgyn. Das poetische Geschlecht und sein Aktus." In *Frauen - Weiblichkeit - Schrift*. Ed. Renate Berger *et al.* Berlin: Argument, 1985, pp. 119-129.

Annas, Pamela. "New Worlds, New Words: Androgyny in Feminist Science Fiction." *Science Fiction Studies*, 5 (1978) pp. 143-156.

Atwood, Margaret. "Marge Piercy: *Woman on the Edge of Time, Living in the Open*." In *Second Words - Selected Critical Prose*. Boston: Beacon Press, 1982, pp. 272-278. Originally published in *The Nation*, 4 December 1976, pp. 601-602.

Badami, Mary Kenny. "A Feminist Critique of Science Fiction." *Extrapolation*, 18 (1976), pp. 6-19.

Bain, Dena C. "The 'Tao Te Ching' as Background to the Novels of Ursula K. LeGuin." In *Ursula K. LeGuin*. Ed. Harold Bloom. New York, New Haven, Philadelphia: Chelsea House Publishers, 1986, pp. 211-224.

Barbour, Douglas. "Wholeness and Balance in the Hainish Novels of Ursula K. LeGuin." *Science Fiction Studies*, 1,3 (1974) pp. 164-173.

-----. "Wholeness and Balance: An Addendum." *Science Fiction Studies*, 2,3 (1975), pp. 248-249.

Barr, Marleen, ed. *Future Females: A Critical Anthology*. Bowling Green, Ohio: Bowling Green State University Popular Press, 1981.

-----. "Charles Bronson, Samurai, and Other Feminine Images: A Transactive Response to *The Left Hand of Darkness*." In *Future Females: A Critical Anthology*. Ed. Marleen Barr. Bowling Green, Ohio: Bowling Green State University Popular Press, 1981, pp. 138-154.

Barr, Marleen, and Nicholas D. Smith, ed. *Women and Utopia: Critical Interpretations*. Lanham, New York, London: University Press of America, 1983.

Bartkowski, Frances. *Feminist Utopias*. Lincoln and London: University of Nebraska Press, 1989.

Baruch, Elaine Hoffman. "'A Natural and Necessary Monster': Women in Utopia." *Alternative Futures*, 1979, pp. 29-48.

Baumann, Hermann. *Das doppelte Geschlecht: Studien zur Bisexualität in Ritus und Mythos*. Berlin: Reimer, 1955, rpt. 1986.

Beauchamp, Gorman. "Themes and Uses of Fictional Utopias: A Bibliography of Secondary Works in English." *Science Fiction Studies*, 4 (1977), pp. 55-63.

Berger, Renate, Monika Hengsbach, Maria Kublitz, Inge Stephan, and Sigrid Weigel, ed. *Frauen - Weiblichkeit - Schrift*. Berlin: Argument, 1985.

Berman, Jeffrey. "Where's all the Fiction in Science Fiction?" In *Future Females: A Critical Anthology*. Ed. Marleen Barr. Bowling Green, Ohio: Bowling Green State University Popular Press, 1981, pp. 164-176.

Betsky, Celia: "*Miss Herbert (The Suburban Wife)* by Christina Stead, *Woman on the Edge of Time* by Marge Piercy." *The New Republic*, 9 October 1976, pp. 38-40.

-----. "Talk with Marge Piercy." *The New York Times Book Review*, 24 February 1980, pp. 36-38.

Bickman, Martin. "LeGuin's *The Left Hand of Darkness*: Form and Content." *Science Fiction Studies*, 4,1 (1977) pp. 42-47.

Bloom, Harold, ed. *Ursula K. LeGuin.* New York, New Haven, Philadelphia: Chelsea House Publishers, 1986.

Brown, Barbara. "*The Left Hand of Darkness*: Androgyny, Future, Present, and Past." In *Ursula K. LeGuin.* Ed. Harold Bloom. New York, New Haven, Philadelphia: Chelsea House Publishers, 1986, pp. 225-233.

Bucknall, Barbara J. "Androgynes in Outer Space." In *Critical Encounters: Writers and Themes in Science Fiction.* Ed. Dick Riley. New York: Ungar, 1978, pp. 56-69.

Building Feminist Theory: Essays from QUEST. New York, London: Longman, 1981.

Chesler, Phyllis. "The Amazon Legacy." In *The Politics of Women's Spirituality.* Ed. Charlene Spretnak. Garden City, N.Y.: Anchor Press/Doubleday, 1982, pp. 97-113. Excerpted from "The Amazon Legacy: An Interpretive Essay." *Wonder Woman/Ms.*, 1972.

Clareson, Thomas, ed. *Voices for the Future II.* Bowling Green, Ohio: Bowling Green State University Popular Press, 1978.

Corea, Gena. *The Mother Machine.* New York: Harper & Row, 1985.

Cornillon, Susan Koppelman, ed. *Images of Women in Fiction: Feminist Perspectives.* Bowling Green, Ohio: Bowling Green State University Popular Press, 1973.

Daly, Mary. *Gyn/Ecology: The Metaethics of Radical Feminism* (1978). London: The Women's Press, 1979.

Donovan, Josephine. *Feminist Theory: The Intellectual Tradition of American Feminism.* New York: Ungar, 1985.

DuPlessis, Rachel Blau. "The Feminist Apologues of Lessing, Piercy, and Russ." *Frontiers*, 4,1 (1979), pp. 1-8.

Ecker, Gisela. "The Politics of Fantasy in Recent American Women's Novels." *Englisch-Amerikanische Studien*, 3 (1984), pp. 503-510.

Edition Schwarze Kirschen 1. *Anarcha-Feminismus.* Berlin: Libertad-Verlag, 1979.

Eisenstein, Hester and Alice Jardine, ed. *The Future of Difference.* Boston: Barnard College Women's Center, G.K. Hall, 1980.

Evechild, Nancy, Margot Rideau, Beverly Adams, and Mary Hastings. "Anarcha-Feminismus - Eine Darstellung." In *Anarcha-Feminismus.* Edition Schwarze Kirschen 1. Berlin: Libertad-Verlag, 1979, pp. 7-20. Originally published as "Anarcha-Feminism - Two Statements," in *Anarchist Review*, 1,3 (1977).

Firestone, Shulamith. *The Dialectic of Sex: The Case for Feminist Revolution.* New York: Bantam, 1970.

Friend, Beverly. "Virgin Territory: Women and Sex in Science Fiction." *Extrapolation*, 14 (1972) pp. 49-58.

Galbreath, Robert. "Holism, Openness, and the Other: LeGuin's Use of the Occult." *Science Fiction Studies*, 7 (1980), pp. 36-48.

Gauster, Hannelore. "Zur Hermaphroditen-Darstellung in der Antike." In *Frauen - Weiblichkeit - Schrift*. Ed. Renate Berger *et al.* Berlin: Argument, 1985, pp. 79-98.

Gearhart, Sally Miller. "Womanpower: Energy Re-Sourcement." In *The Politics of Women's Spirituality*. Ed. Charlene Spretnak. New York: Anchor/Doubleday, 1982, pp. 194-206. Originally published in *Womanspirit*, 2,7 (1976).

-----. "The Future - If There Is One - Is Female." In *Reweaving the Web of Life: Feminism and Nonviolence*. Ed. Pam McAllister. Philadelphia: New Society Publishers, 1982, pp. 268-284.

-----. "Future Visions: Today's Politics: Feminist Utopias in Review." In *Women in Search of Utopia*. Ed. Ruby Rohrlich and Elaine Hoffman Baruch. New York: Schocken Books, 1984, pp. 296-309.

Göttner-Abendroth, Heide. "Der unversöhnliche Traum - Utopie in der Neuen Linken und in der Frauenbewegung." *Ästhetik und Kommunikation*, 10,37 (October 1979), pp. 5-15.

-----. *Für die Musen*. Frankfurt a.M.: Zweitausendeins, 1988.

-----. "Melpomene - Tragödie des Eros." In *Für die Musen*. Frankfurt a.M.: Zweitausendeins, 1988, pp. 92-102.

Gunew, Sneja. "Mythic Reversals: The Evolution of the Shadow Motif." In *Ursula K. LeGuin*. Ed. Joseph D. Olander and Martin Harry Greenberg. New York: Taplinger Publishing Company, 1979, pp. 178-199.

Hansot, Elisabeth. *Perfection and Progress. Two Modes of Utopian Thought*. Cambridge, Mass., and London: The MIT Press, 1974.

Hayles, N.B. "Ambivalence and Assimilation in *The Left Hand of Darkness*." In *Ursula K. LeGuin*. Ed. Joseph D. Olander and Martin Harry Greenberg. New York: Taplinger Publishing Company, 1979, pp. 97-115.

Heilbrun, Carolyn G. *Toward a Recognition of Androgyny*. New York: Alfred A. Knopf, 1973.

-----. "Androgyny and the Psychology of Sex Differences." In *The Future of Difference*. Ed. Hester Eisenstein and Alice Jardine. Boston: Barnard College Women's Center, G.K. Hall and Co., 1980, pp. 258-266.

Heuermann, Hartmut, and Bernd Peter Lange, ed. *Die Utopie in der angloamerikanischen Literatur: Interpretationen*. Düsseldorf: Schwann-Bagel, 1984.

Heuermann, Hartmut, ed. *Der Science-Fiction Roman in der angloamerikanischen Literatur: Interpretationen*. Düsseldorf: Bagel, 1986.

Hillegas, Mark R. "The Literary Background to Science Fiction." In *Science Fiction: A Critical Guide*. Ed. Patrick Parrinder. London, New York: Longman, 1979, pp. 2-17.

Holland, Norman N. "You, U.K. LeGuin." In *Future Females: A Critical Anthology.* Ed. Marleen Barr. Bowling Green, Ohio: Bowling Green State University Popular Press, 1981, pp. 125-137.

Howard, June. "Widening the Dialogue on Feminist Science Fiction." In *Femininst Re-Visions. What Has Been and What Might Be.* Ed. Vivian Patraka and Louise A. Tilly. Ann Arbor: The University of Michigan, Women's Studies Program, 1983, pp. 64-93.

Huckle, Patricia. "Women in Utopias." In *The Utopian Vision: Seven Essays on the Quincentennial of Sir Thomas More.* Ed. E.D.S. Sullivan. San Diego: San Diego State University Press, 1983, pp. 115-136, 253-255.

Huntington, John. "Public and Private Imperatives in LeGuin's Novels." *Science Fiction Studies,* 2,3 (1975), pp. 237-243.

Jameson, Frederic. "World-Reduction in LeGuin: The Emergence of Utopian Narrative." *Science Fiction Studies,* 2,3 (1975), pp. 221-230.

Jefferson, Margo. "Future vs. Present. " *Newsweek,* 14 June 1976, pp. 52-53.

Keinhorst, Annette. *Utopien von Frauen in der zeitgenössischen Literatur der USA.* Frankfurt a.M : Peter Lang, 1985.

Kerkhoff, Ingrid. "Zwischen New Left und New Right: Zur amerikanischen Frauenbewegung 1967-1987." In *Ameri(k)ka: The Sixties.* Ed. Lawrence Gunter, Dieter Herms, and Ingrid Kerkhoff. Berlin: Argument, 1987, pp. 38-61.

Kessler, Carol Farley. "The Heavenly Utopia of Elizabeth Stuart Phelps." In *Women and Utopia: Critical Interpretations.* Ed. Marleen Barr and Nicholas D. Smith. Lanham, New York, London: University Press of America, 1983, pp. 85-95.

Ketterer, David. "Ursula K. LeGuin's Archetypal 'Winter Journey.'" In *Ursula K. LeGuin.* Ed. Harold Bloom. New York, New Haven, Philadelphia: Chelsea House Publishers, 1986, pp. 11-21. Taken from Ketterer's *New Worlds for Old.* New York: Anchor, 1974.

-----. "In Response." *Science Fiction Studies,* 2,2 (1975), pp. 139-145.

Khanna, Lee Cullen. "Women's Worlds: New Directions in Utopian Fiction." *Alternative Futures,* 4, 2/3 (1981), pp. 47-60.

Khouri, Nadia. "The Dialectics of Power: Utopia in the Science Fiction of LeGuin, Jeury, and Piercy." *Science Fiction Studies,* 7 (1980), pp. 49-60.

Kimball, Gayle, ed. *Women's Culture: The Women's Renaissance of the Seventies.* Metuchen: Scarecrow, 1981.

Klein, Gérard. "Discontent in American Science Fiction." *Science Fiction Studies,* 4 (1977), pp. 3-13.

-----. "LeGuin's 'Aberrant' Opus: Escaping the Trap of Discontent." *Science Fiction Studies,* 4 (1977) pp. 287-295.

114

Kress, Susan. "In and Out of Time: The Form of Marge Piercy's Novels." In *Future Females: A Critical Anthology*. Ed. Marleen Barr. Bowling Green, Ohio: Bowling Green State University Popular Press, 1981, pp. 109-122.

Kumar, Krishan. "Primitivism in Feminist Utopias." *Alternative Futures*, 4, 2/3 (1981), pp. 61-66.

Ladenson, Joyce. "Surviving in a Man's World." *U.S.A. Today*, 108 (January 1981), pp. 60-62.

Lake, David J. "LeGuin's Twofold Vision: Contrary Image-Sets in *The Left Hand of Darkness*." *Science Fiction Studies*, 8 (1981), pp. 156-163.

Lao-tzu/Laotse. *Tao te king*. Trans. Richard Wilhelm. Köln: Diederichs, Gelbe Reihe, 1978.

LeBow, Diane. "Rethinking Matriliny Among the Hopi." In *Women in Search of Utopia*. Ed. Ruby Rohrlich and Elaine Hoffman Baruch. New York: Schocken Books, 1984, pp. 8-20.

Lees, Susan. "Motherhood in Feminist Utopias." In *Women in Search of Utopia*. Ed. Ruby Rohrlich and Elaine Hoffman Baruch. New York: Schocken Books, 1984, pp. 219-232.

Lefanu, Sarah. *In the Chinks of the World Machine: Feminism and Science Fiction*. London: The Women's Press, 1988.

LeGuin, Ursula K. "A Citizen of Mondath." In *The Language of the Night*. Ed. Susan Wood. New York: G.B. Putnam's Sons, 1979, pp. 25-30. Originally published in *Foundation*, 4 (1973).

-----. "Dreams Must Explain Themselves." In *The Language of the Night*. Ed. Susan Wood. New York: G.B. Putnam's Sons, 1979, pp. 47-56. Originally published in *Algol*, 21 (1973).

-----. "The Stalin in the Soul" (1973). In *The Language of the Night*. Ed. Susan Wood. New York: G.B. Putnam's Sons, 1979, pp. 211-221.

-----. "Why Are Americans Afraid of Dragons?" In *The Language of the Night*. Ed. Susan Wood. New York: G.B. Putnam's Sons, 1979, pp. 39-45. Originally published in *PNLA Quarterly*, 38 (1974).

-----. "Ketterer on *The Left Hand of Darkness*." *Science Fiction Studies*, 2,2 (1975), pp. 137-139.

-----. American SF and the Other." *Science Fiction Studies*, 2,3 (1975), pp. 208-210.

-----. Preface to 'The Day Before the Revolution.'" In *The Wind's Twelve Quarters*. New York: Harper & Row, 1975, p. 232.

-----. "Introduction to *The Left Hand of Darkness*" (1976). In *The Left Hand of Darkness*. New York: Harper & Row, 1st ed. 1969, rpt. 1980, pp. vii-x.

-----. "A Response to the LeGuin Issue." *Science Fiction Studies*, 3,1 (1976), pp. 43-46.

-----. "Science Fiction and Mrs. Brown." In *The Language of the Night*. Ed. Susan Wood. New York: G.B. Putnam's Sons, 1979, pp. 101-109. Originally published in *Science Fiction at Large*. Ed. Peter Nicholls. New York: Harper & Row, 1976.

-----. Myth and Archetype in Science Fiction." In *The Language of the Night*. Ed. Susan Wood. New York: G.B. Putnam's Sons, 1979, pp. 73-81. Originally published in *Parabola*, 1,4 (1976).

-----. "Is Gender Necessary?" In *The Language of the Night*. Ed. Susan Wood. New York: G.B. Putnam's Sons, 1979, pp. 161-169. Originally published in *Aurora: Beyond Equality*. Ed. Vonda McIntyre and Susan J. Anderson. Greenwich, CT: Fawcett, 1976. A commented version has been reprinted in Ursula K. LeGuin, *Dancing at the Edge of the World: Thoughts on Words, Women, Places*. New York: Grove Press, 1989, pp. 7-16.

-----. "Do-It-Yourself Cosmology." In *The Language of the Night*. Ed. Susan Wood. New York: G.B. Putnam's Sons, 1979, pp. 121-125. Originally published in *Parabola*, 2,3 (1973).

-----. "Talking About Writing." In *The Language of the Night*. Ed. Susan Wood. New York: G.B. Putnam's Sons, 1979, pp. 195-200.

-----. *The Language of the Night: Essays on Fantasy and Science Fiction*. Ed. Susan Wood. New York: G.B. Putnam's Sons, 1979.

-----. "On Teaching Science Fiction." In *Teaching Science Fiction: Education for Tomorrow*. Ed. Jack Williamson. Philadelphia: Owlswick Press, 1980, pp. 21-25.

-----. *Dancing at the Edge of the World: Thoughts on Words, Women, Places*. New York: Grove Press, 1989.

Levin, Jeff. "Ursula K. LeGuin: A Select Bibliography." *Science Fiction Studies*, 2,3 (1975), pp. 204-208.

-----. "Bibliographic Checklist of the Works of Ursula K. LeGuin." In *The Language of the Night*. Ed. Susan Wood. New York: G.B. Putnam's Sons, 1979, pp. 237-270.

Magill, F.V., ed. *The Contemporary Literary Scene 1973*. Englewood Cliffs, N.J.: Salem Press, 1974.

Malin, Lisa. *Die schönen Kräfte: Eine Arbeit über Heilen in verschiedenen Dimensionen*. Frankfurt a.M.: Zweitausendeins, 1986. Originally accepted as Dissertation at the University of Vienna under the title "Die Aporetik des Heilens."

Martinez, Julio. "General Bibliography." In *The Utopian Vision: Some Essays on the Quincentennial of Sir Thomas More*. Ed. E.D.S. Sullivan. San Diego: San Diego State University Press, 1983, pp. 177-233.

McAllister, Pam, ed. *Reweaving the Web of Life: Feminism and Nonviolence*. Philadelphia: New Society Publishers, 1982.

Martyna, Wendy. "Beyond the 'He/Man' Approach: The Case for Nonsexist Language." *Signs*, 5 (1980), pp. 482-493.

-----. "The Psychology of the Generic Masculine." In *Women and Language in Literature and Society*. Ed. Sally McConnell-Ginet et al. New York: Praeger, 1980, pp. 69-78.

McConnell-Ginet, Sally, Ruth Borker, and Nelly Furman, ed. *Women and Language in Literature and Society*. New York: Praeger, 1980.

McGuirk, Carol. "Optimism and the Limits of Subversion in *The Dispossessed* and *The Left Hand of Darkness*." In *Ursula K. LeGuin*. Ed. Harold Bloom. New York, New Haven, Philadelphia: Chelsea House Publishers, 1986, pp. 243-258.

Moulton, Janice, George M. Robinson, and Cherin Elias. "Sex Bias in Language Use: 'Neutral' Pronouns That Aren't." *American Psychologist*, 33,11 (1978), pp. 1032-1036.

Moylan, Tom. "Beyond Negation: The Critical Utopias of Ursula K. LeGuin and Samuel R. Delany." *Extrapolation*, 21,3 (1980), pp. 236-253.

Myers, Victoria. "Conversational Technique in Ursula K. LeGuin: A Speech-Act Analysis." *Science Fiction Studies*, 10 (1983), pp. 306-315.

Neuer Berliner Kunstverein, ed. *Androgyn: Sehnsucht nach Vollkommenheit*. Katalog zur Austellung 17. November 1986 - 4. Januar 1987. Berlin: Reimer, 1986.

Nudelman, Rafail. "An Approach to the Structure of LeGuin's SF." *Science Fiction Studies*, 2,3 (1975), pp. 210-220.

Olander, Joseph D., and Martin Harry Greenberg, ed. *Ursula K. LeGuin*. New York: Taplinger Publishing Company, 1979.

Parrinder, Patrick, ed. *Science Fiction - A Critical Guide*. London, New York: Longman, 1979.

Patai, Daphne. "Utopia for Whom." *Aphra*, 5,3 (1974), pp. 2-16.

-----. "British and American Utopias by Women (1836-1979): An Annotated Bibliography, Part I." *Alternative Futures*, 4, 2/3 (1981), pp. 184-206.

-----. "Beyond Defensiveness: Feminist Research Strategies." In *Women and Utopia: Critical Interpretations*. Ed. Marleen Barr and Nicholas D. Smith. Lanham, New York, London: University Press of America, 1983, pp. 148-169.

Patraka, Vivian and Louise A. Tilly, ed. *Feminist Re-Visions: What Has Been and What Might Have Been*. Ann Arbor: The University of Michigan, Women's Studies Program, 1983.

Pearson, Carol. "Women's Fantasies and Feminist Utopias." *Frontiers*, 2,3 (1977), pp. 55-61.

-----. "Coming Home: Four Feminist Utopias and Patriarchal Experience." In *Future Females: A Critical Anthology*. Ed. Marleen Barr. Bowling Green, Ohio: Bowling Green University State Popular Press, 1981, pp. 63-70.

-----. "Of Time and Revolution: Theories of Social Change in Contemporary Feminist Science Fiction." In *Women in Search of Utopia*. Ed. Ruby Rohrlich and Elaine Hoffman Baruch. New York: Schocken Books, 1984, pp. 55-61.

Piercy, Marge. "The Grand Coolie Damn" (1969). In *Sisterhood is Powerful: An Anthology of Writings from the Women's Liberation Movement*. Ed. Robin Morgan. New York: Vintage Books, 1970, pp. 473-492.

-----. "Mirror Images." In *Women and Culture: The Women's Renaissance of the Seventies*. Ed. Gayle Kimball. Metuchen: Scarecrow, 1981, pp. 187-194.

Plank, Robert. "Ursula K. LeGuin and the Decline of Romantic Love." *Science Fiction Studies*, 3,1 (1976), pp. 36-43.

Porter, David L. "The Politics of LeGuin's Opus." *Science Fiction Studies*, 2,3 (1975), pp. 243-248.

Rabkin, Eric S. "Determinism, Free Will and Point of View in *The Left Hand of Darkness*." In *Ursula K. LeGuin*. Ed. Harold Bloom. New York, New Haven, Philadelphia: Chelsea House Publishers, 1986, pp. 155-169.

Remington, Thomas J. "The Other Side of Suffering: Touch as Theme and Metaphor in LeGuin's Science Fiction Novels." In *Ursula K. LeGuin*. Ed. Joseph D. Olander and Martin Harry Greenberg. New York: Taplinger Publishing Company, 1979, pp. 153-177.

Rhodes, Jewell Parker. "Ursula LeGuin's *The Left Hand of Darkness*: Androgyny and the Feminist Utopia." In *Women and Utopia: Critical Interpretations*. Ed. Marleen Barr and Nicholas D. Smith. Lanham, New York, London: University Press of America, 1983, pp. 108-120.

Riley, Dick, ed. *Critical Encounters: Writers and Themes in Science Fiction*. New York: Ungar, 1978.

Rohrlich, Ruby and Elaine Hoffman Baruch, ed. *Women in Search of Utopia*. New York: Schocken Books, 1984.

Russ, Joanna. "The Image of Women in Science Fiction." *Red Clay Reader*, 7 (1970), pp. 35-40.

-----. "The Subjunctivity of Science Fiction." *Extrapolation*, 15 (1973), pp. 51-59.

-----. "What Can a Heroine Do? or Why Women Can't Write." In *Images of Women in Fiction: Feminist Perspectives*. Ed. Susan Koppelman Cornillon. Bowling Green, Ohio: Bowling Green State University Press, 1973, pp. 3-20.

-----. "'What If . . . ?' Literature." In *The Contemporary Literary Scene 1973*. Ed. F.V. Magill. Englewood Cliffs, N.J.: Salem Press, 1974, pp. 197-201.

-----. "Towards an Aesthetic of Science Fiction." *Science Fiction Studies*, 2,2 (1975), pp. 112-119.7

-----. Women and SF: Three Letters." *Science Fiction Studies*, 7 (1980), pp. 232-236.

-----. "Reflections on Science Fiction - An Interview with Joanna Russ." In *Building Feminist Theory: Essays from QUEST*. New York, London: Longman, 1981, pp. 243-250.

Sale, Roger. "*Woman on the Edge of Time*." *The New York Times Book Review*, 20 June 1976, p. 6.

Sargent, Pamela. "Women in Science Fiction." *Futures* (October 1975), pp. 433-441.

Sauter-Bailliet, Theresia. "Marge Piercy: *Woman on the Edge of Time*." In *Die Utopie in der angloamerikanischen Literatur: Interpretationen*. Ed. Hartmut Heuermann and Bernd Peter Lange. Düsseldorf: Schwann-Bagel, 1984, pp. 349-370.

Scholes, Robert. *Structural Fabulation: An Essay on Fiction of the Future*. Notre Dame: University of Notre Dame Press, 1975.

-----. "The Good Witch of the West." In *Structural Fabulation: An Essay on Fiction of the Future.* Notre Dame: University of Notre Dame Press, 1975, pp. 77-99.

Scholes, Robert, and Eric S. Rabkin. *Science Fiction: History, Science, Vision.* New York: Oxford University Press, 1977.

Spencer, Jane. Introd. *Millenium Hall.* By Sarah Robinson Scott. London: Virago, 1986, pp. i-xv.

Spretnak, Charlene, ed. *The Politics of Women's Spirituality: Essays on the Rise of Spiritual Power Within the Feminist Movement.* Garden City, N.Y.: Anchor/Doubleday, 1982.

Sullivan, E.D.S., ed. *The Utopian Vision: Seven Essays on the Quincentennial of Sir Thomas More.* San Diego: San Diego State University Press, 1983.

Suvin, Darko. "On the Poetics of the Science Fiction Genre." *College English*, 34,3 (1972), pp. 372-383.

Theall, Donald F. "The Art of Science Fiction: The Ambiguous Utopian Dialectics of Ursula K. LeGuin." *Science Fiction Studies*, 2,3 (1976), pp. 256-264.

Thiele, Peter. "Yin und Yang." In *Androgyn: Sehnsucht nach Vollkommenheit.* Ed. Neuer Berliner Kunstverein. Berlin: Reimer, 1986, pp. 251-245.

Tower Sargent, Lyman. "Women in Utopia." *Comparative Literature Studies*, 10,1 (1973), pp. 302-316.

-----. "An Ambiguous Legacy: The Role and Position of Women in the English Utopia." In *Future Females: A Critical Anthology.* Ed. Marleen Barr. Bowling Green, Ohio: Bowling Green State University Popular Press, 1981, pp. 88-99.

-----. "A New Anarchism: Social and Political Ideas in Some Recent Feminist Eutopias." In *Women and Utopia: Critical Interpretations.* Ed. Marleen Barr and Nicholas D. Smith. Lanham, New York, London: University Press of America, 1983, pp. 3-33.

Trömel-Plötz, Senta. "Sexismus in der englischen Sprache." *Englisch-Amerikanische Studien*, 2 (1980), pp. 189-204.

Tschachler, Heinz. "Ursula LeGuin, *The Left Hand of Darkness* (1969)". In *Der Science-Fiction Roman in der angloamerikanischen Literatur: Interpretationen.* Ed. Hartmut Heuermann. Düsseldorf: Bagel, 1986, pp. 295-314.

Tymn, Marshall B. "Ursula K. LeGuin: A Bibliography." In *Ursula K. LeGuin.* Ed. Joseph D. Olander and Martin Harry Greenberg. New York: Taplinger Publishing Company, 1979, pp. 241-246.

Vivelo, Frank Robert. *Cultural Anthropology Handbook: A Basic Introduction.* New York et al.: McGraw-Hill Book Company, 1978.

Walker, Jeanne Murray. "Myth, Exchange and History in *The Left Hand of Darkness.*" *Science Fiction Studies*, 6 (1979), pp. 180-188.

Walker, Paul. "Ursula K. LeGuin: An Interview." *Luna Monthly* (March 1976), pp. 1-7.

Weinbaum, Batya. "Twin Oaks: A Feminist Looks at Indigenous Socialism in the United States." In *Women in Search of Utopia*. Ed. Ruby Rohrlich and Elaine Hoffman Baruch. New York: Schocken Books, 1984, pp. 157-167.

Wilhelm, Richard, trans. *I Ging, Text und Materialien*. Köln: Diederichs, Gelbe Reihe, 1973.

-----. Introd. *Tao te king*. By Laotse. Köln: Diederichs, Gelbe Reihe, 1978, pp. 9-37.

-----. "Kommentar - Die Lehren des Laotse." In *Tao te king*. By Laotse. Köln: Diederichs, Gelbe Reihe, 1978, pp. 127-196.

Wood, Susan. "Discovering Worlds: The Fiction of Ursula K. LeGuin." In *Voices for the Future II*. Ed. Thomas Clareson. Bowling Green, Ohio: Bowling Green State University Popular Press, 1978, pp. 154-179.

INDEX

AACHEN BRITISH AND AMERICAN STUDIES

Edited by Richard Martin and Rüdiger Schreyer

Monika Shafi

Utopische Entwürfe in der Literatur von Frauen

Bern, Frankfurt/M., New York, Paris, 1989. 135 S.
Utah Studies in Literature and Linguistics. Vol. 30
Herausgegeben von Wolf A. von Schmidt
ISBN 3-261-04191-9   br. DM 34.--/sFr. 28.50

Frauen scheint das utopische Wünschen und Phantasieren schwer zu fallen, da sie in Leben und (Utopie-) Literatur vor allem durch männliche Zuweisungen geprägt werden. Zeitgenössische Autorinnen versuchen daher eine andere, von weiblichen Lebenszusammenhängen beeinflußte Utopiepraxis zu entwickeln. Diese 'Utopie des Alltags' wird im literaturgeschichtlichen Kontext interpretiert und als innovativer weiblicher Utopieentwurf begriffen.

Aus dem Inhalt: Das weite Feld der Utopie – Feministische Literaturwissenschaft und Utopie – Christa Wolf: Kassandra – Utopie als Alltag und Vision – Irmtraud Morgner: Amanda – die Suche nach dem weiblichen Orplid.

Verlag Peter Lang Frankfurt a.M. · Bern · New York · Paris
Auslieferung: Verlag Peter Lang AG, Jupiterstr. 15, CH-3000 Bern 15
Telefon (004131) 321122, Telex pela ch 912 651, Telefax (004131) 321131
– Preisänderungen vorbehalten –